MURDO F. C
11A PORTNA G

CU00657060

Rivers
of
Living Water

Rivers
of
Living Water

Rivers of Living Water
All *new* material in this edition
copyrighted by SeedSowers Publishing House
Printed in the United States of America
All rights reserved

Published by The SeedSowers
P.O. Box 3317
Jacksonville, FL 32206
1-800-228-2665

Library of Congress Cataloging - in - Publication Data

Sparks, T. Austin
Rivers of Living Water
ISBN 0-940232-85-5
1. Spiritual Life   1. Title

Times New Roman 12pt

Rivers
of
Living Water

by
T. Austin-Sparks

Preface

T. Austin-Sparks is one of the great figures of the twentieth century who ministered outside of the organized church. For over forty years he held forth at Honor Oak in London, England. The conferences he spoke at, both in Europe and America, have had a profound influence on our time.

Brother Sparks published over one hundred books and pamphlets. The majority of them have ceased to be available to the Christian family. This has been a great loss, as the content of his message has placed him in the category of only a few men of the last one hundred years.

T. Austin-Sparks and Watchman Nee, more than any other men, have influenced the lives of believers who are outside traditional churches. We have felt very strongly that all of brother Sparks' books and pamphlets should be brought back into print if at all possible.

Read T. Austin-Sparks. It is our hope that in republishing his works, his ministry will take wings again, and the influence of his word will spread across the English-speaking world. Hopefully this will give his message a greater influence than ever before.

We send this book forth with a prayer that what he ministered will become realties in the 21st century.

The SeedSowers

CONTENTS

CHAPTER ONE

THE RIVER OF LIFE

OUR KEY SCRIPTURE will be found in the Gospel by John, chapter vii, verses 37 — 39:

" Now on the last day, the great day of the feast, Jesus stood and cried, saying, If any man thirst, let him come unto me, and drink. He that believeth on me, as the scripture hath said, out of him shall flow rivers of living water. But this spake he of the Spirit, which they that believed on him were to receive : for the Spirit was not yet given ; because Jesus was not yet glorified."

The part of that paragraph to which we are giving special attention is the phrase : *" rivers of living water ".*

Around that I want to gather some other passages of Scripture.

First of all in the book of Genesis, chapter ii, verse 10:

" And a river went out of Eden to water the garden ; and from thence it was parted, and became four heads."

Then in the prophecies of Ezekiel, chapter xlvii, verse 1:

" And he brought me back unto the door of the

*house ; and behold, waters issued out from under the
threshold of the house eastward, for the forefront of
the house was toward the east : and the waters came
down from under, from the right side of the house,
on the south of the altar."*

Let your eye run on down the chapter to refresh
your memory on the particulars connected with that
river.

We pass from there to the Gospel by John again,
chapter iv, verse 14 :

*" But whosoever drinketh of the water that I shall
give him shall never thirst ; but the water that I shall
give him shall become in him a well of water springing
up unto eternal life."*

And finally, the book of the Revelation, chapter xxii,
verses 1, 2 :

*" And he showed me a river of water of life, bright
as crystal, proceeding out of the throne of God and of
the Lamb, in the midst of the street thereof. And on
this side of the river and on that was the tree of life,
bearing twelve manner of fruits, yielding its fruit every
month : and the leaves of the tree were for the healing
of the nations."*

"Rivers of living water". John's comment on those
words of Jesus, you note—a comment written long
after Jesus uttered the words, with all the full and long
experience of the Apostle behind the comment—was :

" This spake he of the Spirit, which they that believed on him were to receive: for the Spirit was not yet given ; because Jesus was not yet glorified." The first part of that comment gives the key to the meaning and the nature of rivers in all the Scriptures. It is the Holy Spirit. If we take all these references to rivers and wells, springs and flowing water, to which I have just turned you, as symbolic of the Holy Spirit, then we have certain quite simple and clearly defined thoughts of God.

GOD'S INTENTION FOR HIS PEOPLE

To begin with, this, and not the contrary, is God's mind for His people. God's intention is that the Holy Spirit should be as " rivers of living water." That is the mind of God. Anything other than that is either short of, or contrary to, the mind of God. The Bible begins with this, and the Bible ends with this. In a certain sense, the whole Bible is gathered into this: God's thought and God's mind is that which is meant by rivers of living water. That is, all this represents the great disposition of God to give—what we may call the ' givingness ' of God. God is set forth as one who desires to give, whose inclination is to give, and to give abundantly. That is the simple, basic fact about God, to be taken hold of by faith.

Sometimes, when we are away in a hot country and we are going to have that very delightful function, a picnic, it is necessary for us to find water. But if we have had long experience in the matter we do not just go searching round for water. We lift up our eyes to see where there is verdure, foliage, and we know that water will not be far away : so we make for the verdant foliage and, sure enough, we usually find a stream. And you can always tell where the Lord really is, or has been, by the, so to speak, spiritual verdure, by the greenery, by the foliage. The Lord leaves His mark in that way ; that is His disposition, His very character.

This, then, is God's mind ; and, from the Scriptures which we have read, we infer certain other things about that mind of God, very simple things. God's mind for the individual believer is this : " If *any man* thirst . . . *He* that believeth . . . out of him shall flow rivers of living water . . ." That is in the singular. The thought of God for us, individually, is that out from us shall flow rivers of living water. The individual side is so clearly noted in the Lord's talk with the woman at the well of Sychar—" shall become *in him* a well of water springing up unto eternal life."

But this is His thought for the Church also. In the last chapters of the book of the Revelation, we have the city brought into view, with the river " in the midst of the street thereof ". If this is a symbolic presentation of the Church, as verily we believe it to be, then God's vision for the Church at the end, toward which He is working all the time, is that out from it to the nations shall go this overflow of fulness, this effluence, this river of the water of life. And what is true of the

Church as a whole, universally, is of course intended to be true of every local expression of it. God's idea for every company of His people, wherever they may be, is that out from them shall go rivers of living water. You notice the correspondence between the book of the Revelation and the book of Genesis. In Genesis we read that the Lord God planted a garden (Gen. ii. 8). In Revelation: " To him that overcometh . . . will I give to eat of the tree of life, which is in the paradise of God " (Rev. ii. 7). The last chapters of the Revelation give us to see the tree of life by the river of the water of life. So that the garden in Genesis is a foreshadowing of the Church, a foreshadowing of the paradise of God : God's eternal thought of something out from which His rivers shall go.

OUTFLOW THE SECRET OF INFLOW

Let us be very clear about this : if we, individually or collectively, locally or universally, lose our outflow, we lose the justification of our existence! This matter of outflow must be most jealously guarded. The peril is to draw in, to draw toward ourselves, not only individually, but also collectively. What a vast amount of energy and activity and enterprise and what-not is expended upon trying to get people to come, trying to fill some place, trying to collect and make something! Look at all the attractions that are set up, all the efforts made, to bring, to bring—to bring to some place, or to

some thing, and to build that up. That is the common
way, is it not? Indeed, no other way seems to be known.
But that is not God's way ; that was never God's order.
You cannot find anything like that in the Bible. God's
way is this: pour out, and you will get—it will come
back.

The Martin Luther film that was shown in London
in 1954 was preceded by a film showing some of the
sketches of that great artist Leonardo da Vinci. The last
phase of the film showed the last absorbing occupation
of his life. We are told that in his last years he was
almost entirely taken up with water, water, water—
deluges and floods of water, coming down in terrific
torrents, with terrific force. It caught his artist's imagination and drew his pencil. But one thing that struck
me (especially as I had this present word in mind) was
this: that water, flowing out and pouring out in great
volumes and torrents, when it reaches a certain limit,
recoils upon itself and comes back with equal force, in
great waves that roll over and over one another. It is
easy to understand how all the beautiful light and shade,
swirls and eddies and so on, would catch the imagination of an artist. But this was what came to me from it :
if you pour out enough, in great enough volume, in
great enough strength, it will come back; it will all
come back in overflowing waves.

The Lord put this in another form: " Give, and it
shall be given unto you "; and He went on: " good
measure, pressed down, shaken together, running over,

shall they give into your bosom " (Luke vi. 38). It is a
principle, you see, of God—a principle for life. Do you
want to receive, do you want fulness, do you want enlargement? Do you want all that this means—" rivers
of living water "? It will come from giving ; it will be
the return from pouring out. Of course, you have to
have something to pour out, something to give ; but
that just brings us back to the Divine thought, and to
this statement. I am so happy to think of John, this old
man, after his long life of ministry, work and service,
at last taking up those words of the Lord Jesus, and saying, ' This is what He meant!' Read into that all that
it implies. An old man, who you might think is a spent
force—he has been giving all these years, and might
now be running out—he says, at long last, ' *This* is
what Jesus meant! The Holy Spirit would be in the
believer like rivers of living water, pouring out.' God
grant that we may be like that to the last, never running dry.

This is the Lord's mind, and this is the real nature
of service. It is the secret of life. If we draw toward ourselves, we become an end in ourselves. But if we are
turned outward and are always seeking from the Lord
that which we can give, it will be to our own enrich-
ment and enlargement. It is the secret of life. It is the
secret of service. See, from the day when the river
opened in Jerusalem—the day of Pentecost—the ' givingness' that characterized everybody. Peter and John,
going up to the Temple and seeing the lame man, who

asked an alms, said: "Silver and gold have I none; but what I have, that *give* I thee" (Acts iii. 6). It is the disposition to *give* that characterized the Church at the beginning, because the river had broken out.

There is a story told about Thomas Aquinas and the Pope of his time, Pope Innocent II. Thomas went in to the Pope one day, and found him counting a large sum of money. The Pope said, ' You see, Thomas, the Church can no longer say, "Silver and gold have I none"'. ' No ', said Thomas sadly, ' neither can it say, " Rise up and walk." '

It is the effect of the outgoing, not just the selfish gratification of the incoming, that is the real secret of life and service. If we, individually or collectively, try to draw to ourselves, things will become artificial: that is, *we* shall have to do everything, and we shall be extended to all our wit and ingenuity. But if we are of the disposition to give, to pour out, to see that others get the value, it will not be artificial—it will be spontaneous.

CHARACTERISTICS OF LIVING WATER

Now what we have been saying has all to do with function, the function of the Spirit, the function of the Church, the function of the individual believer, to be a poured forth fulness of God. We go on to say a little about the nature of this life, this ministry; that is, about the characteristics of the Spirit as water. They are very simple ; here they are. The definition is that it is *living* water : that is, that the effect of the life of the believer and of the Church, locally and worldwide, is to create conditions of life, to make for ' livingness ' ; and that is always the test of values. That is always the ultimate proof of truth. The ultimate proof of truth is not rational—that is, we cannot argue it out, and by argument bring somebody to be convinced that we are right. The ultimate proof of truth is *vitality* ; not just what it is in itself, even though it may be truth, but its effect. And the effect of the truth is always intended to be life : life and truth go together. The proof of everything is in the ' living ' conditions which may result, can result, and, if given opportunity, will result. The Lord's intention, then, is that our presence, the sum of our life, should mean that others live and that living conditions—conditions of life—have been created.

Another evidence of the river is *fertility*. I need not take you to all the Scriptures ; they leap to the mind at once. Fertility is an essential feature or characteristic of living water. We have in the Bible one instance, at least, of water that was not living—what we might call ' dead water ' (II Kings ii. 19 – 22). It lacked some element, and the result, you will remember, was that all the fruit fell before it ripened—nothing reached its intended end and purpose. It was dead water ! And the men of Jericho said, ' The water is evil, is bad '. Well, the prophet put that right.

What are we giving? are we giving dead water, so

that nothing goes on and gets through and gets to
maturity? That is not God's thought. Living water
means fertility ; it means productiveness and reproduc-
tiveness ; it means abundance. "Upon the bank of the
river were very many trees" (Ezek. xlvii. 7). "*Very
many* trees". That is God's thought—that you and I
shall leave this scene with a testimony left behind in
many 'trees', in many lives, that God has been this way
and the water has reached those lives through us. That,
again, must be true both individually and collectively.

Further, *freshness*. Living water is fresh water. The
fruit of the tree borne every month declares freshness,
does it not? It almost seems as if nothing were allowed
to get old. Old age, or 'oldness', if I may use an archaic
word, was forestalled, anticipated. Before there was a
chance for it to make itself felt, something fresh was
produced.

There are other illustrations and metaphors in the
Scriptures of this same principle of newness and renewing. We read about 'mounting up with wings as
eagles', 'running and not being weary', 'walking and
not fainting'. That, as you know, is introduced by this :
"Even the youths shall faint and be weary" (Is. xl.
30, 31). So this is something that is not natural. You
look for running without weariness, and walking without faintness, in youth ; but here is something that is
different from that, superior to that—there is newness,
freshness, renewing, all the way along. "They that
wait upon the Lord shall renew their strength." This

is something presented to us for faith's apprehension. Again, *persistence*. The word is: "*rivers* of living water", and there is a tremendous persistence about a great river. I have seen the Euphrates and the Tigris, whose beginnings are referred to in Genesis ii. 10. What an immense volume is coming down there, carrying everything before it, almost terrible in its force and power, allowing nothing to stand in its way, persisting, persisting, persisting, irresistible. When we transfer this from the symbol to that which it symbolizes, we can, of course, understand the Holy Spirit being like this—rivers of living water that will go on and on and on again. But remember that what we are really called to realise is that this has to be *in us*, and then has to go *out* from within us. Thank God for the repeated and again repeated renewings of the Holy Spirit to keep us going on! Thank God for His persistence! Where should we have been but for the Holy Spirit? Where should we be to-day but for this persistence? He comes on and He comes on again.

We note another thing: the presence of health-giving trees by the river. "The leaves of the tree were for the healing of the nations." Here is living water with its *health-giving* properties. How much there is in the Word about the Holy Spirit's work of bringing about healthy conditions! We could spend much time with that alone. The Holy Spirit will, if He has His way, always bring about healthy conditions. All the evil maladies and diseases of a spiritual kind which afflict the Church will be carried away when the Spirit has free course. Unhealthy conditions only say that the Holy Spirit is being hindered somewhere. This fulness of Divine life should make us together healthy people spiritually, full of vigour, full of vitality.

And then: "There is a river, the streams whereof make glad the city of God" (Ps. xlvi. 4). There is *gladness* by the river.

THE CHALLENGE

Now this is all very simple ; it is only a beginning, a foundation. But it is a challenge—indeed, it may be a rebuke. Does it rebuke you? It rebukes my heart ; it challenges, it calls ; it says, 'This is what the Lord wants, and this is what the Lord has provided for, and this is what the Lord does when He has His way.' But I refer you to the Lord's own word: "If *any* man . . . He that *believeth* on me . . ." It is the challenge to faith : do you believe that this is possible with you—with *you*? Do you believe it can yet be, in you? Is this just a general, beautiful, grand idea, but which passes by you personally, and you cannot see or think how it can be true of you? The Lord Jesus simply says to you, personally: "He that believeth . . ." Do you feel dry, dried up? Faith can change that situation. And it is not just *faith*, mark you, which changes the situation ; it is faith *in what God has said*. It is something that faith lays hold upon—something for you to take hold of by faith. " He that believeth . . . out of him shall flow rivers . . ."

Further, the challenge is this, as I said earlier : If this is not true of us as the Lord's people, individually and collectively, the justification for our claiming to be the Lord's people is not there. It seems to me that that is the heart of the Lord's challenge and rebuke to the churches in Asia at the beginning of the book of the Revelation. Some of them had become smug and self-satisfied and self-sufficient ; some of them had just been turned in upon themselves in other ways. The challenge seems to have been that the rivers were not going out. ' If the rivers are not going out', the Lord says, ' there is no justification for you claiming to be a church, a people of God.' But the comfort, the encouragement, is that, if God has shown it to be His will, and if He has made it the very justification of our existence, and has certainly made provision in that He has given His Spirit—and He gives His Spirit without measure—then it can be, *it can be !*

I believe that the Lord desires the recovery of this in His people in a new way. But we must always be very sure of our ground ; and one thing we must be sure about is : Does the Lord mean it? can we really prove that the Lord means that, that that is the will of God? If only I can be fully assured that a thing is the will of God, then I have something to go on—indeed I can go ahead. And here it is. The Lord has shown that He is a God of ' givingness' in no mean or small degree, and that He wants to pour Himself through us—just pour Himself through us. "Out of him shall flow rivers of living water": that is His desire. May our meditations together have that result, so that all the dry channels shall become full, all the parched land shall become saturated, all the low ebb of spiritual life shall give place to a full tide; and in a new way, although we know ourselves to be altogether insignificant people, individually and collectively, yet it will be known that the Lord has passed *this* way. It is not too much to say that there could be enlarged measures unto the nations, unto the very ends of the earth, because of what the Lord does in us. Let us hold on in faith for that.

CHAPTER TWO

THE RIVER AND THE HOUSE

WE TURN NOW to what is one of the most difficult books in the Bible, and yet to my mind one of the richest. It is the book of the prophecies of Ezekiel. Let us read, to begin with, chapter i, verses 1, 4, 5a, 15, 16, 20, 22, 26 ; and then chapter xlvii. Note that this latter chapter follows straight on from chapter xlvi. The first verse of this forty-seventh chapter, *"He brought me back unto the door of the house "*, takes us back to what has gone before as to the House ; and now the writer proceeds: *". . . and behold, waters issued out from under the threshold of the house eastward, for the forefront of the house was toward the east : and the waters came down from under, from the right side of the house, on the south of the altar."* And then again you need to glance on to the rest of the chapter, and then into the last chapter, chapter xlviii. We shall refer to all this as we go on.

Let us now just remind ourselves of the key phrase to all our present meditations, in the Gospel by John —John vii. 37 : " On the last day, the great day of the feast, Jesus stood and cried, saying, If any man thirst, let him come unto me, and drink. He that believeth on me, as the scripture hath said, out of him shall flow rivers of living water. But this spake he of the Spirit,

which they that believed on him were to receive: for
the Spirit was not yet given ; because Jesus was not yet
glorified."

" Rivers of living water." In approaching the book of
Ezekiel, it is necessary for us to be quite sure about one
thing, namely, that the prophecies of Ezekiel really do
contain a message for our own time—for us, now ; not
just that they contain little fragments which are interesting and can be helpful, but that there is here embodied God's message for us. Now, if it is true that
Ezekiel has any present value, it can only be spiritual.
There is much history here, and there is much prophecy,
and prophecy was in the course of being fulfilled while
Ezekiel was ministering ; but it is of great importance
to realise that, in any case, however these prophecies
are interpreted, whether as historical, prophetical, or
spiritual, the historical and the symbolical are but a
temporal representation of the spiritual. That is so
in any case. I am aware of the different schools of interpretation of these prophecies, and I say this with
that knowledge. The spiritual is there in any case, and
it is *the* important thing. The historical will come and
pass ; the prophetical may, or may not, have a literal
fulfilment ; but the spiritual is the eternal and the spiritual is the essential. Hence, we find in Ezekiel not just
an imaginary, but a true, representation of that which
obtains, in principle, in a spiritual way in this dispensation. That has to be seen as we proceed, and it will not
be difficult, I think, to make it quite clear.

THE RIVER RELATED TO THE THRONE

Now Ezekiel said that he " saw visions of God ". We ask, then, what did he see? He saw Heaven opened ; through the opened Heaven he saw a throne, and above the throne the likeness of a Man upon it. That was in Heaven. Then he saw something between Heaven and earth : the medium of the administration of that throne in relation to this world, symbolized in fire, in ' living ones ' (the word ' creatures ' does not exist in the original), and in wheels. From that point onward, there is a long series of messages with illustrations, parables, signs, to carry them home ; then a house, and a river, and the land apportioned for inheritance ; and finally, a city, with the last word, " The Lord is there ". Now, even with that simple, broad outline, it is not difficult for the discerning to perceive that this relates to something more than just history and temporal things. There are clearly here matters of spiritual significance.

In these studies, we are mainly concerned with the river—" rivers of living water ". And yet it is impossible to take the river just by itself, for the river is related to all the rest. It is related to the throne ; it is related to the house, for it comes out of it ; and it is related to the land, for it waters it. So the river can only be appreciated and understood, and known in its value and meaning, as we see it related to these other things.

We shall begin, then, by contemplating the river in relation to the throne and the house. And lest you

should be getting mental pictures and abstract ideas, let
me remind you again of John's comment upon the
words of Jesus about the " rivers of living water "—
that He referred to the Holy Spirit ; and it is really the
Spirit about whom we are talking, though using the
symbols. That comment of John brings us very near to
what we have here in Ezekiel. You know that John and
his Gospel take up one of the resemblances of the
" living ones ". The ' eagle ' aspect of the Cherubim is
that which John brings out. I am not pursuing that now,
because we shall come on it again. My point at the
moment is that John's message is closely related to what
we have in Ezekiel. Here is the starting point: " This
spake he of the Spirit, which they that believed on him
were to receive: for the Spirit was not yet given ;
because *Jesus* was not yet *glorified*." You have to come
first of all to the Man in the throne before you can have
the river. This comment of John, in which he chose the
name, ' Jesus ', introduces at once this inclusive and all-
governing wonder and reality—the Divine idea as to
man. It is a *man* upon the throne, or " the likeness as
the appearance of a man upon it above ", and John says,
" *Jesus* was not yet glorified ", choosing the title of His
humanity, the manhood name of Jesus.

Which leads to this, that the Divine idea as to Man
—firstly with a capital ' M ', and then afterward with a
small ' m '—is that through Him the Divine fulness
should be poured out unto all His inheritance. Think of
that! That God should have ordained to pour Himself

out, in all His fulness, to His inheritance, through man! That is wonderful! If you turn to Ephesians i. 20, you find this: ". . . he wrought in Christ, when he . . . made him to sit at his right hand in the heavenlies, far above all rule, and authority, and power, and dominion, and every name that is named, not only in this world, but also in that which is to come: and he put all things in subjection under his feet"—there is your Man on the throne—" and gave him to be head over all things to the church, which is his body, the fulness of him that filleth all in all." Now you know what is in this Ephesian letter in this connection: first, Christ on the throne ; next, the house—the Church, as His Body —the one new man, the corporate man of which He is head ; and then, from Him, into it and through it, His fulness, rivers of living water.

THE RIVER RELATED TO THE HOUSE

To appreciate and understand the river, we must recognize certain other things which Ezekiel brings out so clearly as to the house. For the house is bound up with the river, and the river is bound up with the house. It is very wonderful—we shall touch upon this in another connection at some other time—but if you make a sketch of this house, as Ezekiel presents it, you will have first of all the great area of the house, which is square, every side equal, and then, coming within that great area, you have the outer court of the house, and then the inner court of the house, and then the house itself in its own divisions. Now, if you take that square of the whole area, and draw diagonals from corner to corner, what will you find right in the very centre of everything, just where they intersect? You will find the altar, with the river flowing out. We will leave the altar for the moment, because that is another matter; but, as you see, the river comes right from the very centre of everything—it is central, and therefore it is related to, and reaches out to, all else. This is the Holy Spirit, working in relation to everything.

(A) THE HOUSE REVEALED

Now look at Ezekiel. First of all, we have the Spirit *revealing* the house. You know how frequently the Spirit is referred to in these prophecies: He is absolutely predominant—it is all by the Spirit: " The Spirit lifted me up . . . ", " the Spirit took me up . . . ", " the Spirit took me away . . . " ; all the activity of the Spirit. First of all, then, the Spirit revealing the house.

Before the real meaning of the fulness of life can be known and entered into, or manifested and expressed, it is necessary for the House of God to be in clear view. The Holy Spirit has to do first of all with the House of God. That is what He has come for. That is the Spirit's object in this dispensation. Be careful not to be swung away from *the* object of this dispensation! There are all sorts of other interesting and fascinating things, about the future and other matters, which are not the present object of the Holy Spirit, and people are caught with the fascination of these side-lines and side-shows. They become occupied with them and are led right off the track of the Spirit's specific movement in this dispensation. Let it be understood that it is the Church, the House of God, which is the Spirit's object, and that we shall not come into the value and benefits of the full tide of the Spirit, unless we are in line with the Spirit's object, the House of God.

That, of course, carries much with it, but the first movement is the Spirit showing the House to the servant of God. It is a very great thing, a very important thing, a very vital thing to be able to recognize the Spirit's object in this dispensation. Everything else, as far as it can be, must come into line with that. Even in a piece of work for God, a valuable piece of work, a good piece of work, a commendable piece of work, if it becomes something in itself, in a circle of its own, unrelated to the central object, and not vitally a part of the Spirit's full intention in this dispensation, there will not be known that fulness of the Spirit that the Lord desires to be known, and those activities of the Spirit which belong to this dispensation.

(B) THE HOUSE MEASURED

The second thing is *measuring* the house. What a lot of detail there is! Every smallest part is measured, and its measurement is fastened upon it. The Spirit is detailing the House of God, bringing the great conception of the House of God down to a detail. Now, it is something to get a great idea or conception or knowledge of the Church—such as the Apostle Paul had, for instance —but even Paul brings that down to details, and very small details they may seem to be. Yet, inasmuch as they are related to the House, they cannot be small. There is nothing that is ' private ', there is nothing that belongs to some other realm, in the life of those who comprise the House of God. Every detail matters! Why stay and give so much time, take so much pains just to give attention to this little piece here, that little fragment there, and to measure it and put its measurement upon it? Why not comprehend it all and just say that the whole thing is *so* big? But the Spirit is meticulous, the Spirit is careful, the Spirit takes account of everything; He overlooks nothing. If we are careless, if we are slipshod about our relationship to the Lord's people, and to the Lord's purpose and the Lord's interests, the Holy Spirit is not. In so far as we are careless, we frustrate the Spirit, we limit the Spirit, and, because He is the Spirit of life, we do injury to our own life.

Paul, who is the great master-builder, deals with so many details, does he not, in every sphere of life—or rather, shall we say, the Spirit through Paul does so. And we *must* come to the Word of God ; it is so important. Do read your Bible, and read it carefully! How often have I said this, that you can often see good Christian people who are obviously violating the Scriptures, in different ways. There is something that the Scripture says, and here is something that is an absolute contradiction. Why? Not because they are deliberately doing it. They have not read the Scriptures! The Holy Spirit gave the Word, and He is jealous about every bit of it. If you and I are really under the government of the Holy Spirit, we shall be checked up on details. Blessed be God, He is within us, and He is the enablement to attend to details.

(C)   THE HOUSE ORDERED OR ARRANGED

Next, we find the Spirit *ordering* the house, just saying where this belongs and what the place of that is, and what the particular function of this is. Everywhere He is defining place and function and relationships. To Him it is all one complete whole, making one Divine order. There is nothing independent, and there is nothing out of harmony; it is all one beautiful, symmetrical whole. The House of God is an order.

Now you understand why I said that introductory word. For there is no getting away from this: that, if we are going to know the fulness, as of the river, we have to come under the Holy Spirit's government for order in the House of God. And that does not mean just in meetings! We are the House of God anywhere and everywhere and all the time, and not only when we are together. From the heavenly standpoint,

we are still the House of God even when we are not
together, and we have to come under this order of the
House of God. This cannot be too strongly emphasized,
because it is a very solemn thing, with which so much is
bound up in lives. It means the difference between enlargement and limitation, whether we are governed by
this very orderly Holy Spirit or not. If we get out of our
place, or if we do not get into our place, we are going
to do terrible damage to the House of God, and we are
going to upset the Holy Spirit's entire plan in our particular relationship. Let us be quite sure that we are
where we are because the Holy Spirit Himself has put
us there and has anointed us for that and has made us
know that that is the thing for which He called us. We
have not just drifted into it, wandered into it, assumed
it or come into it in any other way. We know: This is
where the Holy Spirit has put me, in this relationship, in
this circle, in this company, in this place, and, having
put me here, He has some purpose in my being here,
in this place, and it is for me to know what that is and
for me to keep within my measure and fulfil my function, whatever that may be.

And the functions are numerous. How many aspects
there are of this house!—all quite definite, and yet all
related. But it must be the appointing of the Spirit, not
man's appointment. Do not let man—*as* man, as a part
of some organization or institution—appoint you. The
appointment, even though it may come through godly
men, must come as from the Spirit.

(D) THE HOUSE SHOWN OR EXPRESSED

In the fourth place, we see the Spirit commissioning and commanding: " Son of man, *shew* the house to the house of Israel, that they may be ashamed . . . " (Ezek. xliii. 10). This is a *ministry* : you must have seen before you can show. But what is the best way of showing the house? Not talking about it, not thinking of it, but expressing it. What the Lord wants is a presentation of the house. This is the principle, undoubtedly—to have the house actually in expression, here and there and there, so that the people of God can see where the blessing of God is, where the river is flowing and where the life is, where there is spiritual fulness. ' Show it to the house of Israel.' There never was a time, perhaps, when there was a greater need that there should be an *example* of the House of God, where you see the river flowing ; where it is a reality, it is true.

Now, all this is the administration of the Man and the Throne—it is the Spirit operating in relation to the glorified Man in the Throne. " The Spirit was not yet given ; because Jesus was not yet glorified." We can turn that round. John was speaking in the past tense ; that was then ; but he could have added, ' But that is not so now : Jesus is now glorified, and the Spirit is now given.' The Man is in the Throne. God's appointed and chosen vessel or channel of pouring Himself out is that glorified Man, and all this is the Spirit's work: to administer the rights, the headship, the authority and the order of that glorified Man and of that heavenly Throne—I am only talking in ' Ephesian ' terms, as perhaps you realise!

Knowing how careful one has to be in saying certain things, I am fully aware of what interpretation and construction could be put upon what I am going to say. You see, the Throne now is the Throne of a Man—THE Man. God's authority is vested in a glorified Man; Heaven's administration is through a glorified Man. That was God's conception and idea in making man— " Thou madest him to have dominion . . ."—and the Holy Spirit is effecting that. And therefore all this is essential to the river: that is the thing to which I want to keep so closely all the time. All this is essential to the river—the House, the heavenly government concerning the House, the Holy Spirit's sovereign authority in all matters concerning the House. All that the river means relates to the House, to the Church, to the Body of Christ. Where shall we find the sovereign rule of the Man in the glory by the Holy Spirit? If it is not in the Church, it is nowhere. It is essential for us to be on the ground of the House of God.

THE UNITING FACTOR OF THE NAME

Now, of course, this Church, this House of God, is not to be found here on the earth at present in a literal way, according to pattern. It is a heavenly House, it is a spiritual House. But it is a reality; it is not just an idea.

When you and I take corporate ground in the Holy
Spirit, even with one other believer, we have taken what
we may call ' House ' or ' Church ' ground. When we
gather together as a handful, in the Name of the Lord
Jesus—not as something made or brought about by
man, but in the Holy Spirit—we have taken the same
ground. And that could be extended to many more
things. The importance of it is this—that God recog-
nizes such ground. " Where two or three are gathered
together into my name . . ."—not ' have said, Let's
have a meeting, let's set up a fellowship, or a church,
or an assembly '—no, but " are gathered . . . into
my name, there am I . . ." (Matt. xviii. 20). That is
Church ground. The end of that is: " The Lord is
there " (Ezek. xlviii. 35); and wherever that can be
said, that is the House, that is the Church. It is a spiritual thing ; it is not an arranged thing, an organized
thing ; it is not something decided upon, something that
we do ; but, because we are the Lord's and we bear His
Name, which has been called upon us, and because we
gather together in that Name, that uniting Name which
is called upon us, there *He* is. The Name is the great
uniting factor.

There is a word about this in John x. " He calleth
his own sheep by name " (vs. 3). What name? He does
not call His sheep by ' Tom ' and ' Dick ' and ' Harry '
and ' John ' and all the other names that there are ; that
is not what it means. " He calleth his own sheep "—not
' by their names ', but " by name ". What name? The

Gospels had not yet brought in the full meaning ; they were but parables and figures ; and that is the way by which in the Gospels the great truth opening up later is introduced and signified. " The honourable name which was called upon you " (James ii. 7). " Baptized into the name of Jesus " (Acts xix. 5). And we are called by His Name.

I have given before the illustration of something that I saw in the East. On one occasion I was out in a barren, wild place, and I saw some shepherds leading their flocks from various directions, all towards a well ; and when they arrived at the well, all the sheep and some goats with them got completely mixed up together, while the shepherds went off and had a ' pow-wow '. I thought to myself, Well, here is a mix-up : how ever are they going to cope with this, straighten all this out? When they had had their talk, the shepherds simply parted and went in different directions. One shepherd walked right away and left all his flock mixed up with the others. At a conspicuous point he turned, and started using just one call, one note—I suppose it was a name— which I could not imitate. It was just one sound, and he repeated this, and it echoed down to where the sheep were. Then I saw the flock begin to break up, divide up, separate, and all the sheep belonging to this shepherd went up there after him. He had only used one word, one name, and they knew ! He called them—not by all their names—but by one name, and that name united them all, made them a collective whole with that shepherd.

Now that is the literal fulfilment of what Jesus said :
" My sheep hear my voice, and I know them, and they
follow me " (John x. 27). It is the Name which unites
and makes one—*the* Name! That is ' House ' ground,
that is ' Church ' ground. We are bound together by
the Name. If we take that ground, we are in the way of
the Spirit, we are in the way of life. You know the rest
of that passage. " I give unto them eternal life "—it is
the way of life—" and no one shall snatch them out of
my hand "—it is the way of safety (vs. 28). That is all
the meaning of being on what we call corporate ground.
There is immense value and importance in it, both for
safety and for food.

THE RIVER AND RESURRECTION

To come back to Ezekiel, that is the way of the river.
" Rivers of living water." When Jesus used those words,
it was in the Temple, and it was at the Feast of Tabernacles. You know that the Feast of Tabernacles had one
special feature which no other feast had. It had an
eighth day ; none of the other feasts had. The eighth
day was the " last day, the great day of the feast " (John
vii. 37), and it distinguished that feast from all others.
What is the eighth day? It is the Christian first day, the
day of the resurrection. Eight is always the resurrection
number, and the eighth day becomes the first day. Here
you have the law of the octave : eight repeats one. The
eighth day is the first day : it is the day of resurrection

and it is the day of life, fulness of life. " Blessed be the God and Father of our Lord Jesus Christ, who . . . begat us again unto a *living* hope by the resurrection of Jesus Christ from the dead, unto an inheritance incorruptible, and undefiled, and that fadeth not away " (I Peter i. 3, 4). That is the eighth day of inheritance—the day of resurrection—the feast of Tabernacles. It is life, abundant life ; it is " rivers of living water ", in resurrection union with Him by faith.

CHAPTER THREE

THE RIVER AND THE THRONE

"*I saw visions of God*" (*Ezekiel i. 1*).

"*Out of the midst . . . came the likeness of four living ones. And this was their appearance ; they had the likeness of a man. And every one had four faces, and every one of them had four wings. And their feet were straight feet ; and the sole of their feet was like the sole of a calf's foot : and they sparkled like . . . burnished brass. And they had the hands of a man under their wings on their four sides : and they four had their faces and their wings thus . . .*" (*i. 5 — 8*).

"*Now as I beheld the living ones, behold one wheel upon the earth beside the living ones, for each of the four faces thereof. The appearance of the wheels and their work was like unto . . . a beryl : and they four had one likeness : and their appearance and their work was as it were a wheel within a wheel. When they went, they went upon their four sides : they turned not when they went. As for their rings, they were high and dreadful ; and they four had their rings full of eyes round about. And when the living ones went, the wheels went beside them : and when the living ones were lifted up from the earth, the wheels were lifted up. Whitherso-*

ever the spirit was to go, they went; thither was the
spirit to go " (i. 15 — 20).
" And above the firmament that was over their heads
was the likeness of a throne, as the appearance of a
sapphire stone : and upon the likeness of the throne was
a likeness as the appearance of a man upon it above "
(i. 26).
" And he brought me back unto the door of the house ;
and behold, waters issued out from under the threshold
of the house eastward " (xlvii. 1).

W̲E̲ COME NOW to consider the connection of this
" river of water of life " with the throne, and with this
symbolic medium—the cherubim, the wheels—of the
administration of the throne, and with the Man upon it.
We have seen the counterpart of this in the New Testament: Jesus raised and set ' far above all rule, and
authority, principality and power, and every name, not
only in this age, but in that which is to come ' (Eph. i.
20, 21) ; and then, out from Him, the exalted Lord, in
the day of His exaltation and glorifying—the day of
Pentecost—the river flowing right out, by way of and
through the House, the Church, unto the nations. Now,
coming to this river in its relationship to the throne and
what I am calling this symbolic medium of the throne's
administration—living ones, wheels, firmament, the
spirit of life, flashing light and power—we need to be
able to grasp clearly what this has to say to us in our
time.

THE STATE OF THE CHURCH
AFFECTS THE WHOLE CREATION

The book of the Revelation, which contains so much
that is akin to what is in the prophecies of Ezekiel,
throws some light on this matter. The Revelation, as we
know, was written especially in relation to the spiritual
departure and declension of the Church—for everything is bound up with the Church, even the nations and
the kingdom of Satan. These have a large place in that
book, but God begins with the Church, represented in
the churches, and ends with the Church, represented in
the heavenly Jerusalem ; and all that comes between is
related to the Church. That book, then, was written
because of the declension and departure of the Church
from its original position, and it constitutes one tremendous argument that everything depends on the spiritual
state of the Church.

That throws light upon this book of Ezekiel, because
it was written for the very same purpose. Historically, it
is related to the departure, the declension of Israel ; it
was a clear emphasis upon this very same thing. The
nations are affected and involved ; all kingdoms are
bound up with *this*. What happens to *this* people has
an effect upon all other peoples. This creation is a collective whole, and what God has set at the centre of it—
His own people—is something that matters to the whole
creation. Paul makes that very clear and emphatic, when
he says : " the whole creation groaneth and travaileth

in pain . . . "—waiting for what?—" for the revealing of the sons of God " (Rom. viii. 22, 19). The whole creation is involved in this central thing : God's interest in His own people, God's purpose concerning His own people. The people of God are not only central to the Lord's interests, but they affect everything else. The Devil knows that, and we ought to be alive to it. How necessary it is, then, that the Lord should have His people in a right condition, as He intended they should be. It is not possible to exaggerate or over-emphasize the importance of the Church's being in a right condition.

The river of water of life—which, as we have seen from John's comment, is nothing other than the Holy Spirit Himself expressed in fulness—the river of the water of life is, in the first place, related to the people of God, the Church, the House of God, and then *through* them to the nations.The Bible makes that perfectly clear in the beginning, in the book of Genesis : the river running out of the garden in Genesis ii. 10 is here in Ezekiel xlvii. All the land is affected by the river. And in the end, in the book of the Revelation, it is like that. The river runs out, giving life to the tree, and " the leaves of the tree " are " for the healing of the nations " (Rev. xxii. 2). You see, what is inward with the people of God is intended to be available to give character to what is in this world. The Lord's thought is that His people should first of all receive abundantly from Him by the Holy Spirit, and receive so abundantly that they have rivers flowing out from themselves. Of course, the receiving side is a most important one. " If any man thirst, let him come unto me and drink ; " and then, when he has filled himself, " out of him shall flow rivers of living water." I shall not dwell upon that just now— it will come up again ; but this is God's thought and God's provision.

THE CHERUBIM

Coming now to this that I have called ' the medium of the exercise of the throne ' and the flow of the river of life, or the fulness of the Spirit, there are some simple but very important things to note. But first, just a word or two concerning the beings known as the Cherubim. They are mentioned in a full way in the Bible no fewer than eight times, and many more times just by reference. In Genesis they are without the garden, guarding the way ; they are outside. In Exodus they are abiding inside the sanctuary, at rest ; no longer outside, but inside. This carries its own significance, I think, as we may see in a later chapter. In the book of Kings they stand and wait : they are waiting for the king. In Isaiah (ch. vi) they burn and fly. In the book of the Revelation (ch. iv) they sing and worship. In Ezekiel, where they are twice mentioned fully, in chapter i and chapter x, they see and they run—vision and action—taking in the whole situation, and doing something about it. And note that their energy is the energy of the Holy Spirit. The Spirit is in them—the ' spirit of the living ones ' ; and the

Spirit is " in the wheels "—the active power and energy is that of the Spirit, all-seeing, and all-active in relation to what is seen.

THE COUNSEL OF GOD IN OPERATION

Now I am not going to say what the Cherubim are. All sorts of interpretations have been given. The last, I think, and fullest, is that they are symbolic of the Church. I am not even going to say that. But, whatever they are, they are in any case the embodiment of the principles of the throne—the Man in the throne in the exercise of His eternal purpose. Paul sums this all up for us, I think, in one statement: " Who worketh all things after the counsel of his own will " (Eph. i. 11). It is the counsel of God in operation. We should be satisfied with the recognition of that. And what a mighty thing it is! Look at all the features here in this first chapter of Ezekiel's prophecy—the features of action, of livingness. It is abundant life, it is rushing winds, it is noisy wheels, it is many eyes, it is running feet, it is the unturning, undeviating persistence of a straightforward going, it is flashing lightning, it is burning coal, it is clouds and whirlwinds—it is ceaseless action. And what does it all mean? It means tremendous energy. " Who worketh "—and that word ' worketh ' is the Greek verb *energeo*, from which we get our word ' energy '—" who *energizeth* all things after the counsel of his own will ". And through Paul we are given clearly to understand that that is now, in this dispensation. I believe that amongst the many things we need to recover is this one : we need to recover an assurance and confidence and conviction that, how ever things may seem, God is like this in our day ; that, through all things, over all things, behind all things, God is pursuing His counsels—He is going on. Ceaseless in action, undeviating in course, with tremendous energy, He is working all things after the counsel of His own will. Sometimes, as we look out, we wonder if God is doing anything, and in our prayer times we try to get God to do something. What we need is to realise that God *is doing*, and to get into line with His doings. Perhaps He is not doing what we want Him to do, or what we think He ought to do, and in the way in which we think He ought to do it ; He is not employing the means that we think He ought to employ—*our* bit of means, *our* bit of work. He may not just be coming that way, but He is pursuing His purpose, relentlessly, persistently, undeviatingly ; and the need for the people of God is to be brought right into the straight course of His goings from eternity.

For He is going, and He is going in our day ; it can be seen—more or less—in the world. But, seen or not seen, the fact remains—or our Bible is not right, and Paul was mistaken ! And I am glad always to recognize this : that when Paul stopped travelling about the world and had all his tremendous activities among the nations curtailed, it was then that he saw the goings of God from eternity, it was then that he wrote this letter to the

Ephesians, containing the eternal counsels of God. It is a wonderful thing, is it not? When we are taken out of our work, when we cannot run about and do all sorts of things, when we are perhaps physically unable to do anything, God is going on. Sometimes we think that, when we stop, God has to stop, and if we do not go, well, God will not be able to go! Oh, no, He is going on— He is going on! May we be helped to understand His goings, and to get into His goings.

Now, that is what is here in Ezekiel. You have first of all the *medium*: four *living ones*—four aspects. Four is always the number of what is universal. You have the four winds, you have the four points of the compass, you have the four seasons of the year. Everything that relates to what is universal is four. At the end of the Bible we read that the city is foursquare, and on the four sides the gates are open—that is universality of administration, universality of benefit and value. Four is what is universal. God is moving—but not on our smug scale; He is not going to be tied down to our little corner, to be shut up to our little box. God has great universal interests at heart, and we need to be very much enlarged.

Then the *predominant factor* is this: the *Spirit.* "And they went every one straight forward: whither the spirit was to go, they went" (Ezek. i. 12). The Spirit is the predominant factor. He is governing all this.

Thirdly, we have the *inclusive feature*: *man.* There is the Man on the throne, and then there is the man-aspect of the Cherubim. You notice how this is stated:

" they four had the face of a man "—semi-colon ; and
then the other likenesses added. One is that of the lion,
another that of the ox, and another that of the eagle ;
but the face of the man is the dominant feature of this
medium of the Divine counsels. It is concerning man,
it is through man, it is with the man-conception of God
in view. It is a Man who is on the throne. Yes, very
God ; but remember, God has glorified a Man, which
was ever His intention when He made man. He has got
Him there, in glory, and now His counsels are to bring
men into conformity with the image of *that* Man. All
that is happening here is the activity of God to get a
corporate and collective man, corresponding to the Man
who is glorified.

How much there is in that! Your life and mine—
and the energies of God! This is God energetic in our
lives, if only in patience. What tremendous energy there
is behind the patience of God with us! We should not
be able to go on for a day, had not His patience tremendous energy behind it. Thank God, dear friends—
and let us draw all the comfort that there is to be drawn
from these truths and realities—God is going straight
on where we are concerned. I do thank God for that!
Many is the time that I have turned aside, got out of
the way ; I have sought out my juniper trees and flung
myself down under them and said, ' It is enough, O
Lord, take away my life—it is no good.' Many times
we have got like that, out of the way, off the path ; we
have thrown ourselves down, lost heart, because of what

we have found in ourselves, or the difficulties in others, or in the way, or disappointments. And yet, to date, as many times as we have got there, we have come back; somehow or other—not by our own resolve or energy —we have got on our feet, or been put on our feet, and we have gone on for a while longer. It just means this : that God is not giving up, God is going on! My brother, if you are down in despair and disheartenment to-day, that is you—that is not God. God is going on. Believe it, get hold of it: God is going right on, He has not given up yet!

Let us believe this and lay right hold of it. It is like the old cable, you know, upon which the street cars used to run in Glasgow. We had there what was called the ' Subway '—a noisy, rackety old thing—and there was this winding cable that went round the city, and the old cars or trams put down a clutch and got hold of it, and on they went. When they let go they stopped, and when they took hold again, on they went and did the whole circuit. It was just a matter of how long they kept hold. The cable was going, all right, always going, per-petually in motion, but it was a matter of holding on.

God is like that. That is the picture here. God is go-ing on. And He is going straight on, relentlessly, un-deviatingly. Get hold! Now the trouble was that Israel had let go. Israel had let go of God, and was left behind. If we have lost hope, if we have lost heart, may the Lord help us to-day in faith to rise up and lay hold again. Thank God, He has given us of His Spirit! We can

lay hold on the Spirit, and lay hold on life. Is that not
perhaps exactly what Paul meant when he said: "Lay
hold on eternal life" (I Tim. vi. 12)? That life is going on. Here is life, fulness of life, embodied or represented in these Cherubim—and it is going on. If you
prefer the metaphor of the river—dive in and let it
take you! "Lay hold on eternal life."

THE FOUR ASPECTS OF THE CHERUBIM

We turn now to the fourfold expression of the Spirit
—the essentials of the Divine purpose and the Divine
counsel.

First, the *lion* aspect of the medium of God's activity.
Amongst other things which it may say, it certainly
means this: spiritual government and authority. That
wise man, Solomon, said about the lion that he "turn-
eth not away for any" (Prov. xxx. 30). The lion has
never been known to turn round and flee. If he starts,
nothing but death will stop him. The going of the
Spirit is like that. Whether you and I go on or not, it
will make no difference to the going of the Spirit. He
has the eternal counsels of God to execute and to perfect, and He is going on to that end—He is going to do
it. And here the sovereign government and authority of
the Spirit in the counsels of God and in the Church is
essential. There must be this heavenly government, this
heavenly authority, by the Holy Spirit. Everything must
come under Him. That is a statement which ought to

be enlarged upon very considerably. But we can see how true that was at the beginning, from the day of Pentecost onward, for some time. The lion aspect of the Spirit came in to go on—and what government, what authority was found expressed in the Church by the Holy Spirit! It goes ill with anyone who gets in the way of the Holy Spirit.

Then, the aspect of the *ox*. This is certainly, amongst other things, the element or feature of strength, of energy. You will recall that in the temple Solomon made a laver to contain 16,000 gallons of water—a considerable weight. What was chosen to bear that up? Twelve oxen, the symbol of strength. I am not dwelling upon the function of the laver or of the oxen in that connection, but simply upon the fact that they set forth a feature of strength, of energy, to bear responsibility, to carry burdens, to effect purposes. And here is the strength, the energy, the power of the Holy Spirit to effect the purposes of God. " Not by might, nor by power, but by my spirit, saith the Lord of hosts " (Zech. iv. 6). That is almost invidious, is it not? The margin says: "not by an army". An army is man's idea of power, the world's conception of might. But God says, ' No, by my Spirit '—superior to any army, and to all the armies together, in energy, in strength, in power. It must be by the power of the Holy Spirit. Let us seek earnestly that the Lord, the Spirit, may express Himself in greater fulness, as a river of power.

And then, the *man* aspect. This—again amongst

other things—signifies intelligence and understanding. Amongst all created beings, man is really the only one who has this kind of understanding and intelligence. Of course, sometimes we think that some animals have better sense than men!—but in the highest sense man is, or at least was intended to be, the intelligent creature amongst God's creation. Intelligence of understanding is related to manhood. And the Holy Spirit desires to give to you and me, and to the Church generally, His own Spirit of understanding, intelligence and knowledge. How important that is! If the Holy Spirit is going to effect the purposes of God, and if we are to know the Holy Spirit in this fulness as represented by rivers of living water, it is very important, indeed essential, that we have spiritual understanding as to what the purposes of God are. Yes, the Spirit requires that we have intelligence as to what He is really after. A very great deal of strength is being wasted, and much energy expended to no real purpose, in many things that are being done, because they are not directly in line with and on the course of the Spirit's essential purpose. It is no use our just thinking out, planning, and trying to do things for God, according to our own judgment and reason. We have to know what the Spirit is doing—really what He is doing. And so we must have intelligence and understanding in the mind and the ways of the Spirit.

And finally, the *eagle* aspect—what is it? Amongst a number of other things, it undoubtedly means absolute freedom of movement. If you have ever seen an eagle in flight, on the wing, the impression that it has made upon you has been that it is just free. It seems as if the whole universe is at its command: perfect detachment from any kind of limitation and restraint. The Holy Spirit demands that! If we say the Holy Spirit must come *this* way, and do *this* thing, and in *this* manner, we cramp Him and confine Him. The Holy Spirit will ignore us. Peter tried to do that with the Holy Spirit over Cornelius and his household, but the Holy Spirit was not having any of it at all. He beat Peter down to this: 'Recognize this, Peter: I am sovereign—I demand absolute freedom of movement. I am not coming along the line of your interpretations and restrictions and traditions. You come off the earth into the heavens, with Me, and we will move freely.' And did he not? The absolute sovereignty of the Holy Spirit is essential to the fulness of His expression and to the fulness of His life. He demands liberty to move as He will and not according to our ideas and our interests. The absolute sovereignty of the Holy Spirit is basic to the fulness of life.

CHAPTER FOUR

THE RIVER IN RELATION TO THE THRONE AND THE ALTAR

" He brought me back unto the door of the house ; and behold, waters issued out from under the threshold of the house . . ." (Ezekiel xlvii. 1).

" And above the firmament . . . a throne . . . and upon . . . the throne . . . a likeness . . . of a man upon it above " (Ezekiel i. 26).

NOTICE, FIRST OF ALL, that the river coming down from out of the house passed to the south of the altar. In an earlier chapter I pointed out that, if you were to draw a diagram or plan of the whole temple area as it is described in the book of Ezekiel, you would find that that area was a great square, and, if you drew diagonals from corner to corner, the point at which they crossed, right in the centre of the square, would mark the position of the altar. The wall of the whole temple area, as you know, was six cubits wide and six cubits high. You will be impressed with one thing—not for our immediate consideration, although it may take hold of your thoughts—namely, the immensity of the area in comparison with the actual temple, and especially with the inner sanctuary. The temple, or the house, is the thing of intrinsic value and significance—that is, everything is gathered into it ; but the area around it, which it sanctifies or consecrates, is a large area, and so there is a very considerable space between the House of God and the world beyond.

THE SPACE BETWEEN THE CHURCH AND THE WORLD

Let that say to you what it ought to say ! The world ought not to be very near. And the House of God ought not to be very near to the world, in a wrong sense. Some people seem to think that the presence of that distance, that area, that great space of separation, means loss of influence. The nearer you can get to the world, and the more you can bring the world into the Church, the greater is likely to be your effect upon the world— a principle altogether contrary to the Word of God. The Lord Jesus is the very embodiment and personification of the temple of God, the sanctuary of God, the House of God, and there is no doubt about it, that, while He walked in the midst of this world, there was a very great space between Him and it, and no one could cross it except by being born again. The men and women of His day did not even understand Him ! They could not cross in mind, in intelligence, in understanding, or in appreciation. The space was there. He walked with God as in Heaven, while here, and He is the figure of the Church of God. Those same principles obtain within the Church.

Now that is not my subject at the present moment, but it is something to emphasize and it ought to impress us. My point is that that great temple area was there— and you remember the word was: "the whole limit thereof round about shall be most holy" (Ezek. xliii. 12).

Right at the centre, then, of the whole area, where the lines meet, was the altar. It was right at the very centre of everything. That is the word: the absolute *centrality* of the Cross. That is where God has put it, that is where the Scriptures have put it, that is where the apostles put it. It is central to all New Testament teaching, it is central to all New Testament preaching. The one central reality around which the apostles and the first preachers gathered everything was: Christ crucified and risen—the Cross on its two sides, in its twofold aspect. That is a statement of familiar fact; but we must recognize that everything centres in the Cross— the Cross is now the Divine centre of everything.

THE RIVER AND THE ALTAR — THE PLACE OF ASHES

Now this is the point: that the river comes down by the Cross—in other words, the Holy Spirit always comes by way of the Cross. The reason is known to us so well in teaching, in doctrine: but we learn it so slowly in experience, and with so many creaks and groans and grumbles, that the Cross is, on the one side, the place of judgment, where all that is not of the new

creation is brought to ashes. It is the end of everything.
We are slow in learning that because we are so slow in
appreciating it. But we know it. We know that it is the
place of the ashes. There is no life in ashes, no fruit in
ashes, there is no future for ashes. Ashes themselves
speak of an end of everything. And the Cross, from one
side, is the place where all is brought to judgment and
to ashes.

When we were speaking earlier about the features of
the tremendous activities of God as we have them in the
first chapter of Ezekiel's prophecies, you remember that
we noted a combined feature of flashing lightning and
burning fire. In the book of the Revelation, which, we
said, throws so much light upon these prophecies, we
have seven lamps of fire. It is the same principle. The
flashing lightning and burning fire in the one, and the
seven lamps of fire in the other: it is only another way
of picturing the same thing. The flashing lightning, or
the lamp, means making known, uncovering, revealing,
disclosing, searching out and manifesting. The Cross
does that, and it is doing it all the time. And the burning
lamp implies the consuming of what is manifested, of
what is made known. The Cross does that too.

But, on the other side, of course, it is the place of
the new beginning, and from the very ashes there
springs into bloom a new garden. " In the place where
he was crucified there was a garden " (John xix. 41).

With that twofold activity and effect of the Cross, the
Holy Spirit is very greatly concerned. He comes down

as the Spirit of Life by way of the Cross. Leaving the symbols and the pictures and the types and the figures, we know how true that was in reality, in this new dispensation inaugurated on the day of Pentecost. It was a *new* age, a *new* day—the day of being ' begotten again to a living hope by the resurrection of Jesus Christ from the dead ' (I Peter i. 3). They preached Christ crucified on the day that the river came down. What was the ringing note above all other notes in their preaching? " Whom ye crucified, whom God raised " (Acts iv. 10). " Ye crucified . . . God raised "—the story of the Cross in two fragments. The Spirit came on that. Whenever they proclaimed or testified to that, something happened: the Spirit came that way immediately.

And He always does; that is His way. By the Cross He comes and by the Cross He abides. The river may go on, it may go a long way, extend far; its waters may reach far away from that point; but they are never cut off from it, and the course is never diverted to some other part. No matter how far the river goes, no matter how much it accomplishes, no matter how much territory it overruns, no matter how long its history is, it never, either at its beginning, or during its entire course, takes any other way than that of the Cross. What I mean is that the Cross is not merely something that happened, either in history or in experience, at some time in the past—and that is finished, that is done, that is that—it is only being elementary and rather superficial to talk about the Cross when you have been a

Christian for so long. That is not the teaching of the
Word of God. We shall prove to the last moment of our
lives, if we are going on with the Lord, that the Holy
Spirit is still working by means of and by way of the
Cross, and that every fresh experience of the Spirit in
life and fulness will be based upon some fresh application of the principle of the Cross.

THE SIGNIFICANCE OF 'ASHES'

On the one side, there is ashes. Are you knowing anything about ashes? Perhaps you are feeling that everything has gone to ashes. In your own spiritual life for
the moment, your own experience, or perhaps in your
ministry, in the work of God, it is so dry, so unfruitful,
so unprofitable, so barren ; it seems so much like death.
It is like that sometimes. At one moment the river seems
to be flowing at full torrent, and then, somehow or
other, it seems as though the waters have dried up. How
are we to interpret this?

Now—whether we like it or not, whether we understand it or not, whether we know the Scriptures about
it or not—it is true that, in our Christian life and ministry, we have successive experiences of 'ashes'. They
do not come at regular intervals—they are very irregu-
lar ; but they come, and they last for shorter or longer
periods. Sometimes it is very intense and concentrated
into a short time, but it is so terrible that it would not
do for it to go on much longer. Sometimes it extends

over months, or a year, or two years—a time when it all seems to be ashes. Now is this right? That is the question. Should it be like that? Do you say, 'No, certainly not'? Well, I am sorry for you, but I am going to say that it *should* be like that!

Now, such a statement always needs to be covered and protected. Dryness and ashes may be the result of some real hindrance to the Holy Spirit. Then it is wrong—it is not the Lord's thought when it is like that. If we have resisted or disobeyed the Holy Spirit; if we have violated the most conspicuous teaching of the Word of God and its principles; if we have persisted in some way, where the Lord has tried to change us and where, if only we had been ready to let go and not be so strong, things would have been very different: if that has been so, then there will be ashes, but not according to God's will.

If, then, a time of ashes comes, we need to find out whether we have been in self-will, in rebellion, in resistance, in unwillingness to accept what the Lord would have offered or shown; whether in some way we have stood across the path of the Spirit. And, if we are not able to see that we have done that; if, after examining our hearts before the Lord and really getting down in humility, in meekness, in brokenness and in utter openness and pliableness to the Holy Spirit, we can say before God, No, it has not been that; then there is another interpretation, another attitude to take. What does it mean?

Well, as we have said, the principle of the Cross is
an abiding principle: the Holy Spirit never departs
from it. All the way it is like that, and it would seem
that again and again, for reasons known to Himself—
they may become clear to us presently—He finds it
necessary to get something more of the ' carry-over ' of
the old creation out of the way, to make room for a
larger measure of Himself. It is a difficult and painful
process, but it comes that way. We pass through times
of great spiritual suffering and distress, where everything seems to have come to an end. The Spirit wants
greater room ; He is desiring a deeper and a wider
channel. He is acting, not primarily to bring us to an
end, but to get a larger place for Himself in us, to bring
us into a greater fulness of His life, of His power, of
His flow. And it is true to principle, that those channels
which carry the greatest volume of life and help to
others are not shallow ones. They have been ploughed
or dredged deeply ; they have been dealt with in a very
drastic manner.

GOD'S ' GIVINGNESS ' AND MAN'S POSSESSIVENESS

That is for our comfort, our consolation, our encouragement. We can be quite sure of this one thing : that,
even when our hearts are wholly toward the Lord and
there is no self-will and self-strength in His way, there
will be times of ashes. But the Lord's object is to give
" a garland for ashes, the oil of joy for mourning, the

garment of praise for the spirit of heaviness: that they might be called trees of righteousness, the planting of the Lord" (Isa. lxi. 3)—which reminds us of the trees by the river in Ezekiel's vision. The Holy Spirit, who is the river, gives all that ever God wants us to have —and it is a great all—by way of the Cross. We commenced by pointing out that rivers in the Bible—in Genesis, in Ezekiel, in John and in Revelation, and everywhere else—rivers and wells and springs, being types of the Spirit of Life, at least imply, if they do not positively declare, that God is the great Giver. God's thought is to give, to give, to give, not in trickles, but in rivers—rivers of living water. And if God purposes to give like that, we must know that all His giving is governed by the Cross. And all that the Holy Spirit will give, He will give by way of the Cross.

Our flesh wants to *get*. I suppose the deepest-rooted thing in human nature, the very thing that brought about the Fall and all its lamentable consequences, is acquisitiveness or possessiveness. It does not matter who the person is: whether on the positive side—the agressive, determined type ; or on the negative side—the very, very meek nobody, with the ' inferiority complex ', as it is called, which is only another way of looking at this possessiveness. Oh, the self-pity which is born of this wanting to have! Self-pity is a reaction ; it is only, after all, another way of trying to draw to ourselves. Yes, possessiveness is there ; it is universal—it is in us all. It is the deepest thing in our being.

But God, who has all, is just the opposite: *His* whole disposition is to give, to let go. *We* want to have the Lord, to have His blessing, to have the Holy Spirit, to have power—to *have* Divine things. What for? We might repudiate the suggestion that we wanted them for ourselves: but who knows the human heart? only God. And that is why so often, in giving us what He wants to give us, He first of all takes us through an awful time before He does give. He deals with that personal possessiveness until we come to the place where we say, ' Lord, if you do not want me to have it, I don't want it.' That is a good place to be! It is not that we become sulky or recalcitrant; far from it. It is simply this: ' Lord—only if You want it, only if *You* want it. Not for me—for You.' And then the Lord responds. " To this man will I look, even to him that is poor and of a contrite spirit" (Isa. lxvi. 2). The Holy Spirit gives all that He has come to give by way of the Cross.

THE SPIRIT INTERPRETS THE CROSS

The Holy Spirit as Teacher interprets to us the Cross. Is that not true of the ministry in the New Testament? Ministry in and by the Holy Spirit is so largely an interpretation of the Cross. There is the statement of fact about the Cross: Christ died, He was crucified, He laid down His life. But what does it mean? We need the later letters of the New Testament in order to understand what it means. And the Holy Spirit has seen to it that we have in them a very full interpretation of the Cross. We shall not get anywhere unless and until we understand the Cross as interpreted to us by the Holy Spirit.

You see, it was "through the eternal Spirit" that Jesus "offered himself" (Heb. ix. 14). It was by the very leading and enablement and energy of the Holy Spirit that Christ laid down His life. It required the Holy Spirit to do it. It was not just a man giving away his life, consenting to have it taken away; we know that the death of the Lord Jesus was a far, far greater thing than that. It touched the whole range of the satanic hierarchy: it touched the whole range of the creation, which is itself to be delivered from bondage: and it touched the whole range of humanity. It requires the mighty Spirit of God to make a death do that! — and to make a man do that through death. We cannot exaggerate the greatness of the Cross of the Lord Jesus.

But since it was "through the eternal Spirit" that He "offered himself", so, too, only the Spirit who led Him to the Cross, the Spirit who carried Him through, can rightly interpret to us what He meant by the Cross. Men are all at sea about the crucifixion and the death of Christ: they flounder in the utmost confusion in trying to interpret it and put a construction upon it; and yet all this error about the death of Christ is simply because those who propagate it are not Spirit-taught men. If we are taught by the Spirit, we shall come to understand the Cross. No Spirit-guided ministry will ever come to ignore the Cross or make little of it. It will rather do what the Holy Spirit does—keep it in the centre and make everything circle round it.

SPIRITUAL MEN MADE BY THE CROSS

The Holy Spirit makes spiritual men by the Cross. The water has come down by the altar. It flows down through the court and the area, and out beyond, and on the banks of the river are very many trees, and the trees bear their fruit every month. Now trees in the Bible are symbols of men. The Bible speaks of people being trees of the Lord's own planting (Isa. lxi. 3). " He shall be like a tree planted by the streams of water " (Ps. i. 3). These trees, then, are symbolic of men drawing their life from the Holy Spirit and bearing their fruit as the result. They are spiritual men, in the life, the verdure, the fruitfulness of the Spirit.

This is exactly what came about as the result of Pentecost. Spiritual men seemed to spring into being on that day, drawing their life from the river that was flowing. They were men of spiritual measure, of spiritual intelligence. Before the Spirit came, those very men at the centre of things—Peter and James and John, and others—were in the dark, completely befogged! They could not for the life of them see any value in Jesus dying. " Be it far from thee, Lord: this shall never be unto thee " (Matt. xvi. 22): in other words—if this happens, all is lost ; our hopes are disappointed. And those two on the way to Emmaus: what despair, what hopelessness in their conversation, because, as they thought, Jesus had died. None of them could understand at all; it was all death, and dark, dark night.

But on the day of Pentecost they understand it all! They glory in it, and have nothing else to talk about! They have received light on the meaning of the Cross. Now they are spiritual men, in very truth *born-again* men, with spiritual understanding, spiritual intelligence, spiritual influence. I think the wonderful thing in their hearts would have been this: ' Why—do you remember how we could never see a glimmer of hope or light or prospect, if Jesus died? That is how we used to think of it. What an awful thing the Cross was to us! To us it was the symbol of the end of everything, through all time to come. And yet now, here we are— it is the very thing in which we are glorying! Is it not wonderful? That Cross which we thought was going to be our undoing is our making. The Holy Spirit has used the very thing that we feared and dreaded to make new men of us!'

NEW LIFE BY THE CROSS

He brings life everywhere by the Cross—everywhere. " Every thing shall live whithersoever the river cometh " (Ezek. xlvii. 9). Everything shall live—that is the work of the Spirit. Everywhere life coming by way of the Cross. Do not let the Devil shut you up over the Cross, but be careful! If you wrongly interpret and apply the

Cross, it will mean a kind of end that God never meant. If you are always turning in on yourself in an effort to crucify that self of yours, you are applying the Cross in a wrong way. Leave it to the Holy Spirit! You believe God's truth about the Cross; you see what God means by it; and then you turn yourself over to the Holy Spirit, and say: ' I can't do this—You must do it. I am going on—I shall make blunders, I shall make mistakes, I shall slip up, I shall go wrong; I shall have to go to the Lord again and again, and say I am sorry; but will You please be responsible for this— I can't do it!' You see, if you and I take hold of the Cross to try to crucify ourselves, we are going to become subject to terrible introversion. There is a false meaning of the Cross, making for introspection and self-despair, which God never meant. The Cross is intended, not to throw us in upon ourselves, but to deliver us out of ourselves into new life.

THE SPIRIT'S OBJECT A FULL WORK

Now, one word more. The Holy Spirit always aims at a full work. If men stop with what is partial, something serious will happen. If they make any piece of work a thing in itself, something serious will happen. If they make any line of teaching a thing in itself, or if they treat a part of the truth as though it were the whole, something serious will happen. If, for example, we make evangelism the whole thing, something serious will happen! Sooner or later that thing will go underground, and may disappear. This river relates to the *House*: it takes its rise in the House—that is, in Christ and His Church, as one House of God. If you take anything away from that full thought—for the House of God is the *full* thought of God, it is " the fulness of him that filleth all in all " (Eph. i. 23)—if you do not keep things closely related to the House of God, something serious will happen—and does happen. There are big movements, and they are not related to the House of God. You look for them after a time, and where are they? What proportion of them can be traced and found? They have disappeared, they have gone underground. If you make a teaching on the Holy Spirit—Pentecostal or whatever you may call it—something in itself, and do not relate it to the full purpose of God, you will get an awful confusion, deplorable situations and conditions, which are a disgrace to the Lord.

The Holy Spirit works in relation to God's full thought and purpose ; He purposes a full work. It is only as everything is brought into relation to the full purpose and object of God that the Holy Spirit will go on in increasing fulness. He will stop if we put the limit of ' things ' upon Him, whether the things be works or teaching. He will demand a full way in relation to His full purpose. The measure of the Spirit that we know will be proportional to the measure of the purpose of God in our lives. If we are only in a part of what God has purposed and we are not going beyond that part, we shall only have that measure of the Spirit. If we are right in line with the full purpose of God, we shall have the full co-operation of the Holy Spirit.

So the river is related firstly to the Cross, for keeping the way open, deepening and broadening the channel ; and then it is related to the House : because everything in the purpose of God, both in this dispensation and in all the ages, is related to what goes by the name of " the House of God "—the Church—that wonderful, Divine masterpiece that God conceived " before times eternal ". We need to be in that—a big thing indeed—if we are to know a big experience of the Holy Spirit.

CHAPTER FIVE

THE RIVER OF GRACE ABOUNDING

" How precious is thy lovingkindness, O God! and the children of men take refuge under the shadow of thy wings. They shall be abundantly satisfied (margin: "They shall be watered ") with the fatness of thy house; and thou shalt make them drink of the river of thy pleasures " (Psalm xxxvi. 7, 8).

" Whosoever drinketh of the water that I shall give him shall never thirst ; but the water that I shall give him shall become in him a well of water springing up unto eternal life" (John iv. 14).

" Jesus stood and cried, saying, If any man thirst, let him come unto me, and drink. He that believeth on me, as the scripture hath said, out of him shall flow rivers of living water" (John vii. 37, 38).

" And he showed me a river of water of life, bright as crystal, proceeding out of the throne of God and of the Lamb . . ." (Revelation xxii. 1).

" And the Spirit and the bride say, Come. And he that heareth, let him say, Come. And he that is athirst, let him come : he that will, let him take the water of life freely " (Revelation xxii. 17).

Leaving ezekiel for the moment, we turn our
thoughts to the simple meaning of this river of life, and
all the wonderful, Divine promises associated with it.
We begin with a re-statement of the fact that these
things said about the river of life, the river of God—
about the children of men being satisfied and watered,
and being filled and made channels and vehicles of
this life in fulness—all show what the Christian life
is intended to be. We make that simple but positive
affirmation on the authority of very much of God's own
Word. That is how it ought to be, that is how it can be,
and that is what God has provided for. What is it that
makes the Christian life like that?

Again, the Scripture is full of the answer. It is that
God has given His Holy Spirit: and, throughout the
Bible, the symbol of the Holy Spirit as the Spirit of life
is water—not in little drops, but in rivers. "Rivers of
living water", said Jesus ; and John, immediately com-
menting on that, said: "This spake he of the Spirit
. . ." God has sent the Holy Spirit in these terms to
make the Christian life like this. What is the river? It
is the river of life. Said Jesus: "I came that they may
have life, and may have it abundantly" (John x. 10) ;
not in a little trickle, but abundantly. That was His idea
as to the Christian life. What is this fulness of life, this
fulness of the Spirit? The answer is in one fragment
given us by Paul: ". . . that ye may be filled unto all the
fulness of God" (Eph. iii. 19). It is, therefore, the ful-

ness of God ; and the statement is that it is God's will, purpose, intention, that we shall be filled unto all that fulness.

A further question. What is the motive lying behind the giving of this river? What accounts for it, what explains it, by what motive has God been actuated in purposing and providing for this? And the answer is in one word: *grace*. The river is, after all, the river of God's grace. It was to that that this same John referred when, looking back over a long life, the long period that had elapsed since first he came into touch with Jesus, he said: " For of his fulness we all received, and grace for grace " (John i. 16). This is a tumbling river. It is a wonderful thing for an old man of ninety, with all that he had seen of the work of God, and all the people that he had known to come into this grace, to gather it all up in this testimony: ' And we all ' (I wonder who he was thinking of—certainly a great number) ' we have all received of His fulness, grace upon grace.' ' We have all drunk to the full, and have scarcely touched the fringe of this river of grace.' Or think of Paul's words—surely only inundations of water can describe or define what Paul meant, when he said : " . . . where sin abounded, grace did abound more exceedingly " (Rom. v. 20)—the word is " did superabound ". We know what inundations of water are ; we know something of wide-spreading floods in modern times. Yes, sin abounded, but grace abounded so much the more.

EPHESIANS—THE LETTER OF FULNESS

Now, in order to get some idea of what this means, this grace abounding, this river of grace, we are going to turn to a very familiar book—the letter to the Ephesians. You know that this is the document of fulness. This letter is written in superlative upon superlative, a tumbling of language over itself as it strives to cope with the immensities that are in view. The language is the language of the overflowing of fulness. There is the "exceeding abundantly above all that we ask or think" (iii. 20)—one wave succeeds another, overwhelmingly. Again, we find: ' that you may know what is the breadth and the length and the height and the depth, the knowledge-surpassing love of Christ' (iii. 18, 19). It is the letter of Divine fulness for the people of God.

And that Divine fulness is presented in many very wonderful ways. This letter brings to our knowledge and understanding what we can find nowhere else in the Bible: the great thought of God for His people before time was, and the electing, the choosing of that people for Himself, with a great purpose in view. God is coming out from eternity into time to find them, and lifting them out of time and carrying them on into the eternity to be, with great thoughts, great designs, great intentions, great purposes. We have here the wonderful revelation of God's ' pre-thought' about us, of His calling of us in time, and of the great purpose of that thought and that calling, to be realised throughout the ages of ages.

Dear friend, if you have responded to the call of Jesus Christ and to the grace of God, you will find, as you go on, that you are caught up in something tremendous, something immense, something with which you cannot cope. Here Ezekiel comes wonderfully to our rescue, as we attempt to picture what is here. You remember how the river came out from beneath the threshold of the house, flowing by way of the altar, out through the whole sacred area, and down through the land, gaining in breadth and gaining in depth. The prophet says that the man in the vision led him up to the river and then into the river, and at first it was ankle-deep; and then he was led further until it was knee-deep, and still led on until it was thigh-deep; then—" waters to swim in ", and the last description is, " a river that could not be passed through " (Ezek. xlvii. 1 — 5).

That is wonderful! If that is the river of Divine grace, it is more than you and I will be able to compass or master, more than we can bring within our poor, limited capacity. It will be beyond us, always, no matter what the need may be; it will always be beyond us. Have you found that out yet? I am finding that out. Have you never got to the place where you despaired of yourself—where you thought that perhaps the grace of God could not help you any more? But you find that this river is beyond you altogether: you cannot cope with this river of grace! As I was saying, if you respond to the call of grace you will discover that it is something tremendous. It goes right back before time and on after time: it is boundless as eternity.

GRACE THE BASIS OF ALL

Let us, then, look at our letter to the Ephesians. This is the letter, we were saying, of fulness, and the impressive thing about it is this: that one of the most frequently used words in it is the word ' grace '. It is not a long letter—you can read it through in twenty minutes—and you will come on ' grace ' no fewer than twelve times. Let us just see, then, what it has to say about grace in relation to fulness. *" But God . . . even when we were dead through our trespasses, quickened us together with Christ (by grace have ye been saved), and raised us up with him, and made us to sit with him in the heavenlies, in Christ Jesus "* (Eph. ii. 4 – 6). " By grace have ye been saved ". The apostle brackets that, but that is a tremendous thing. " When we were dead "—dead to God, dead to all God's purposes, dead to all the meaning of our very being from God's standpoint; yes, " dead through our trespasses "—He " quickened us together with Christ ". ' But ', the apostle is very careful to say,—' but it was all of grace.' " By grace have ye been saved." That is the basis of everything.

You see, he is going to say some very wonderful things. Almost immediately he is going to launch out into the matter of this eternal fulness. He is going to take us back and he is going to take us on, and he is going to tell us some astounding things about this Christian life. But the basis of it all he puts in here, in brackets, as though to say, ' Let us make quite sure that they do not run on too quickly, but know exactly what the basis of it all is—by grace.' The basis of everything is grace. Let us say quite simply, quite emphatically, that, whatever you do, however long you go on, and hope and struggle and wait, you will never get away from this: it will always be on the basis of grace. And grace is grace —it *is* grace! God has said it is grace—it *has* to be grace, and you will never make it anything else. That is the open door for everything. Grace opens the door, and becomes the very entrance into all this fulness. The river of grace brings us in.

GRACE THE GOAL OF ALL

" . . . *That in the ages to come he might shew the exceeding riches of his grace in kindness toward us in Christ Jesus* " *(ii. 7).* And then a re-affirmation to safe-guard that: " for by grace have ye been saved through faith " (vs. 8). What a statement! I have often said that you can never exhaust this letter. Every little fragment of it will keep you occupied for a lifetime, and that is not exaggerating. Just listen again: " *that in the ages to come he might shew the exceeding riches of his grace in kindness toward us in Christ Jesus* ". Can you grasp that? It is beyond you, it takes your breath away. It defeats and defies every effort to comprehend and understand and explain. But there is the statement. Under the illumination and constraint of this self-same Holy Spirit—the eternal Spirit, who knew everything before ever man was, and knows everything when time shall be no more—this man Paul was led to put that down, as the wonderful goal of grace. " That in the ages to come he might shew the exceeding riches of his grace in kindness toward us in Christ Jesus ". That is the object of all. The basis of all is grace ; the final object of all is grace. Here is the source of the river—grace. Here is the course of the river, picking us up in time —calling us, saving us by grace. Here is the goal of the river—carrying us into the ages to come and making us the very means or vessel of displaying the " exceeding riches of his grace ". How great is the grace of God!

GRACE TO PROCLAIM CHRIST

Let us move to the next chapter. " . . . If so be that ye have heard of the dispensation of that grace of God which was given me to you-ward ; . . . whereof I was made a minister, according to the gift of that grace of God which was given me according to the working of his power. Unto me, who am less than the least of all saints, was this grace given, to preach unto the nations the unsearchable riches of Christ " (iii. 2, 7, 8). Here is

electing grace for service. It was a tremendous thing
that this man was called to do. He was thinking, 'How
great is this calling which God has laid upon me! how
immense is this privilege, this opportunity, this choosing of me—*me*, who am less than the least of all saints!
To think that I should be chosen for it! It is just grace.'

Now, you and I are not Pauls, by any means; we do
not stand in the same category as he. But we have the
same message and the same blessed commission. There is
not one of us who is not called to proclaim the grace of
God to the nations. It may be to the nation into which
we were born and in which we have to remain, it may be
to others; but, as the people of God, as a part of the
Church, the Body of Christ, our function, our business,
our existence is to make known the grace of God. It is
even grace that we should be able to do that! What
tremendous grace it is that any one of us should be
allowed, even in the smallest way, to minister to others
the things of Christ.

Here is the electing grace of God—sovereign grace,
Paul would call it. 'Why choose me? why allow me?
why give this honour to me—to one who is " less than
the least of all saints "?' Can you put yourself into that
category? I think there are some who feel just like that.
Paul did not say, ' less than the least of all preachers, or
teachers ', but: " less than the least of all saints "—of
all Christians. Do you feel like that? Yes: without any
feigned humility at all, without any put-on meekness,
we may well believe ourselves to be like that; we may

feel that we are utterly worthless. But sovereign grace looks toward the most worthless and says: ' It is possible, *even for you*, to know My grace in such measure that you can go and honestly tell others of it without being in a false position, without there being any contradiction whatsoever.'

THE PROVISION OF GRACE

We pass on to the next chapter. " *But unto each one of us was the grace given according to the measure of the gift of Christ* " (iv. 7). Here is grace doing something else. Grace calls us; grace brings us into God's great purposes and thoughts, in direct line with that goal in the ages to come to manifest and show forth " the exceeding riches of his grace in kindness toward us in Christ Jesus "; next, when we are in, grace gives us something to do—some work to do, some message to convey; and then grace stands behind us and makes full provision. " Unto each one of us was the grace given according to the measure of the gift of Christ ": grace is the wonderful provision for all that to which God calls and which He has in view.

How the Apostle knew that grace as the provision! There was a time when he found himself troubled, bothered—indeed, almost annoyed, as well as handicapped and thwarted—by something in his life. It was not some sin, not something morally wrong, but perhaps a physical malady. He described it as ' a mes-

senger of Satan to buffet him ', ' a stake in the flesh '
(II Cor. xii. 7), something that seemed all the time to
be holding him down. And he would say, ' How, how in
all the world can I fulfil my ministry, how can I do all
that God has called me to do, with this thing always
interfering and bothering me? It seems such a contradiction ; it seems to be so inconsistent with the calling
and the possibility. On the one side, I hear a voice that
says : God has called you to this ; and, on the other, I
find that He has given me this terrible handicap in it.'
    Paul was in the throes of that problem, that seeming
paradox. He says : ' I cried to the Lord about it and said,
Lord, take it away—it is a hindrance, it is a limitation.
No answer. And I said again, Lord, take it away ! No
answer. And I came back again the third time—" for
this thing I besought the Lord thrice "—Lord, take it
away. And the Lord did not say, No, I won't. But He
said unto me, " My grace is sufficient for thee : for my
power is made perfect in weakness." Without taking it
away, I will make it possible for you to do all that I
want you to do. You may have limitations, you may
have difficulties ; you may have things which seem to
spell defeat and curtailment ; but grace can enable for
the doing of the thing in spite of them.'
    Those things may be necessary, as Paul came to see,
' lest I should be exalted above measure '. They may be
necessary to keep out pride, which would wreck any
ministry quicker than anything else. Pride will destroy
usefulness to God far more quickly than sickness or in-

firmity or ' messengers of Satan to buffet '. Let us keep that out at any price, and rely on the supply of grace, which will see that the thing is done.

THE INFLUENCE OF GRACE

" Let no corrupt speech proceed out of your mouth, but such as is good for building up as the need may be, that it may give grace to them that hear " (iv. 29). The effect of grace in our lives is to cause us to behave properly, to speak properly ; to be good people, courteous people, gracious people ; to say things which minister grace : so that others, because of the work of grace in us, become gracious also, become characterized by the grace of God. Here is the effect or the influence of grace in our lives. The grace of God working in your life and mine means an influence on others, so that they also come under the influence of that grace and become different.

" Let no corrupt speech proceed out of your mouth ". Because of the work of grace in you, you do not use the words that others do. But it does not end there. Your presence makes other people feel that it is wrong to say that sort of thing, to talk like that, and even ungodly people begin to stop using their corrupt communications in your presence. The grace of God in your life is putting a restraint upon them. And if they do let go, they have a bad time afterwards ! ' I do wish I knew your secret—how it is that you are able to be provoked, to be annoyed, to be upset, and yet not do this sort of thing. You do not let go!' That is a simple beginning of a work of grace in others because of the work of grace in you—the effect of grace upon other people when it is worked in us. "That it may give grace to them that hear". That is the best kind of ministry, is it not?—far better than preaching and talking and telling people that they should or should not do things. Let them see the grace of God, and come under its influence, and they may be changed. Grace is an effective thing. It is not something passive; it is something that tells upon others.

THE BENEDICTION OF GRACE

Finally: *"Grace be with all them that love our Lord Jesus Christ in uncorruptness"* (vi. 24). "Grace be with *all* them . . ." This is a part of what we call the 'Benediction'. "Peace be to the brethren, and love with faith, from God the Father and the Lord Jesus Christ." Yes, but it is a benediction of grace! A benediction is not just a formula to be pronounced at the end of a meeting. A benediction is a blessing to impart. And we ought to be a benediction. We ought to be the very grace of God in this world, the blessing of God to others. It is so easy to pronounce something that we call the 'blessing' or the 'benediction'. But the man who ended his letter like this was not just using pious language, winding up his letter in some nice, proper way. He was himself a

benediction. And you and I have come under the blessing of the grace of God, in this man Paul. Now that
same grace is to us-ward, that we should be a blessing :
not merely that we should pray for a blessing on others,
and not only pronounce blessings on others, but *be* a
blessing—the blessing of the grace of God.

The grace of God is a very great thing : it is mighty
to save, to keep, to use, and to make us a blessing. When
we respond to the grace of God, we find ourselves in
something very great—something that could never,
never be compensated for by anything or everything else
that we might have. And so the Apostle was most concerned, and prayed that believers might not fail of the
grace of God. We pray that, too, concerning any who
may not be the Lord's—that they may not miss the
grace of God. This favour comes out to us freely and—
because it *is* grace—asks for nothing as a basis for operation, calls upon us to do nothing but to accept it in
faith, to believe in the good faith of God. That is all.
You will only put it back if you argue, in any way, ' I
am not good enough '. That puts grace out of court,
does it not?—for grace is just what it is *because* we are
not good enough! We may almost say that it *requires*
us not to be good enough. There would never be such
a thing as grace if we were good enough. Grace pre-
supposes in its very nature that we are not good enough,
and that we can do nothing about it.

Perhaps you argue : ' But if I do start, I shall not be
able to go on '—and you put grace out of court again,

because none of us has ever gone on one day without the grace of God, as we know right well. Grace comes in to keep us going. ' But I could never be of any use to God—oh, no, I could never think that I could serve the Lord.' You put grace out of court when you say that. Ask the people who have been most used by God—ask this man Paul, so mightily used. Was it because he was such a well-educated man, so clever, so intellectual, had such tremendous power of mind and will? He will tell you, ' Certainly not ; none of it would have carried me on. It is nothing but the grace of God that has seen me fulfilling my ministry.' You say, ' Well, I think that great calling, that which you say is going to be at the end, is far beyond me. That might be for some people, but I cannot think that it applies to me.' If you say that, once again you put grace out, for it is grace that is going to do it. It was grace that wrote our name in the Lamb's book of life, and the grace that commenced will perfect.

It is all of grace. Cast yourself upon the grace of God. I am quite sure that some of us who have known the Lord a long time find that this is the only thing to do, and we want to do it again : just plunge into the river and let it carry us on—the river of His grace.

CHAPTER SIX

SPIRIT AND LIFE

"It is the spirit that quickeneth; the flesh profiteth nothing: the words that I have spoken unto you are spirit, and are life" (John vi. 63).

THESE TWO WORDS, spirit and life, denote—firstly, the nature, and, secondly, the effect: spirituality in nature, and life in effect, or as the result.

SPIRITUALITY CREATES A DIVIDE

The context in which these words were actually used shows that they represented, and indeed effected, a divide. It was a divide, firstly, between Christ and the Jews as such; but it was, secondly, a divide between Christ and a number of disciples who were just adherents, ' professors ', outward followers—such as had not been ' added ' to Him in a spiritual way. " No man can come to me, except the Father which sent me draw him " (vs. 44). There was evidently a considerable number of people who added themselves to Him, who joined up with Jesus and went about with Him: wherever you found Him you could always see them—the same old faces, always there, showing some interest—

and yet they had not been added to Him by the Father in a spiritual way, there was no inward change ; and when He began to speak deep spiritual things, they found they could no longer be followers, for they were not disciples *inwardly.* " Upon this many of his disciples went back, and walked no more with him " (vs. 66). They just dropped off. His words, because of their spirituality, found no corresponding spiritual ground, and therefore they created a divide. This is something to take note of and something which might be followed up with a good deal of illumination.

The division was, in the first place, between spirituality and *materialism.* When we speak of ' materialism ', of course we usually think of something gross, something very much of the world of commerce, its results and values in finance and credit and so on—that realm of the mundane ; but it is of much wider application than that. Materialism denotes an outlook that embraces, and at the same time limits itself to, everything that can be seen and handled and appreciated with the natural senses. It is the material as over against the spiritual, the seen as over against the unseen, the temporal as over against the eternal, the earthly as over against the heavenly. It is a very wide term.

It was also the divide between spirituality and *ceremonialism.* Of course, ceremonialism is only an aspect of materialism—the religious aspect of materialism. These very, very ceremonial scribes and pharisees and rulers and priests in Israel were very materialistic, as we know; everything was on the outside. The divide was between all that had to do with the external forms and procedures of religious institutions, and spirituality.

Further, it was the divide between spirituality and *mysticism*: a divide which is very real, but often very difficult to trace and to define. You see, the religion of the Old Testament was so very largely a religion of symbols—we might say that it was entirely presented in a vast and comprehensive system of symbolism. We shall come to that again as we go on. It is so easy to take symbolism and interpret it as mysticism and mistake that for spirituality. All these Old Testament symbols, of which we are going to speak again presently, how mysterious they are! If you like, how mystical they are!—it is only another way of saying the same thing. And then they become fascinating, especially to certain types of mind and temperament, and they are taken up and used and explained. Very often that is done, and the thing remains as a kind of mysterious fascination, and leads nowhere. It is all very wonderful: the very mystery about it is fascinating—it is not all on the surface; and that appeals to certain kinds of people. But what have you got after all your study of types and symbols? what does it amount to? how much real spiritual measure is resulting from it? how much of it all remains just mental enjoyment and pleasure? Mysticism and spirituality are two utterly different things—they belong to two different realms. Mysticism has crept into Christianity and is taken for spirituality—and it is nothing of the kind. It is very important to recognize that and to track it down.

We may sum up by saying that it is the divide between what is of the Spirit and what is of the *soul*— between the spiritual and the *soulish*. Israel's Old Testament religion was entirely of the soul: that is, it was something that could be appreciated by the natural man. He could look on, and could even participate in it, without being a different man ; he could be thoroughly engrossed and absorbed in the thing, so that it was *the* thing above everything else in life, and yet it make no difference to him at all. That is what is of the soul. What is of the Spirit is essentially different from that. It not only belongs to another and different realm ; it has an altogether different effect. The Lord Jesus, in the phrase which we quoted at the beginning, said: " It is the spirit that quickeneth ; the flesh profiteth nothing ". Of course, by " the flesh " He does not mean the body ; that is only His way of saying ' the natural life '. He is saying to these religious people, who had all this of the Old Testament, its form and its symbolism and its typology and everything else: ' In the realm of things spiritual, the soul, the natural life, gets you nowhere.'

SPIRITUALITY—THE TEST AND ' THE TRUTH '

Now, the test of everything religious is: How far does it really reach its end—that of making spiritual men and women, spiritual and living people? The test

of everything is there. All that these religious people,
the Jewish nation, had—and it was a great wealth—
did not make them spiritual people, and did not, therefore, make them living people, in the true sense. The
Lord Jesus, as recorded in this chapter of John, is just
putting his finger on this—that there is a tremendous
gap between all that and true spirituality; and He is
presenting the test. The test of the value of everything
—the test of our Bible knowledge, the test of all the
wealth that we may have derived from Bible study, the
test of all our association with Christian things, the test
of all the work that we may be doing in the Lord's
Name, the test of every institution and every means of
Christian service—rests just here, on one thing only:
How far is it producing spiritual men and women?

This is a very necessary challenge for to-day in Christianity. Christianity, as we know it, can be divided
between truly spiritual men, and those who are not that,
though professedly Christians. Now note that all else—
all that is other than spirituality, or spiritual men and
spiritual women living as Jesus meant by ' living '—is
what He called ' not the truth '. He was constantly making this distinction. This Gospel by John contains the
distinction again and again. The most familiar instance
is that in chapter iv, in His talk with the woman of
Sychar. At a certain point, the conversation having become rather embarrassing—too personal—she changed
the subject, and widened out. Recognising that He was a
' religious man ' and ' wanted to talk religion ', she

decided that she could do that : ' Our fathers worshipped
God in this mountain—you Jews say that God ought to
be worshipped in Jerusalem.' The Lord said: ' Believe
me, woman, the hour is coming and now is when the
true worshippers shall worship neither in this mountain
nor at Jerusalem. God is spirit and they that worship
Him must worship Him in spirit and in truth. Such He
seeks to be His worshippers ' (vs. 21 – 24).

You see, Mount Gerizim, the temple of the Samari-
tans, and Jerusalem, the temple of the Jews, represented
the whole system of religion in that land. This temple
is material ; it is earthly, it is ceremonial ; and Jesus
simply, so to speak, takes the sponge and wipes that
realm right off the slate. He says: ' That is not the
truth ; the truth is only that which is spiritual. That
which is spiritual is the only truth.' " In spirit and
truth ": just go through the Word and see how often
He is pressing that. It is really the essence of chapter vi
of John's Gospel. What is " the truth ", according to
Jesus? It is not all this of which we have spoken. The
truth. is that which in its very nature and essence is
spiritual.

SPIRITUALITY MEANS SEEING

And the first thing about spirituality is to have eyes
—to be able to see. Look at the context of the words
which we quoted at the beginning. " And they said, Is
not this Jesus, the son of Joseph, whose father and

mother we know? how doth he now say, I am come down out of heaven?" (vs. 42). That is an index to a very great deal. You see, these religious people, these responsible religious people, knew Him only in an earthly way—they had not the faintest conception of Him in a heavenly way. He is repeatedly saying, ' I came down from heaven ', ' I am the bread which came down from heaven.' ' Oh ', they say, ' this is all beyond us— this is all nonsense!' It was on that very point that first of all the Jews, and then His disciples, went away from Him. They could not *see* beyond what was earthly and of time ; they only knew in that ' close-up ' way of the flesh, not in a heavenly way at all. This talk about someone coming from Heaven was to them something altogether outside their realm.

Spirituality in its very first feature is seeing. That is clearly shown in the Cherubim, with which we were occupied in earlier chapters. We have not exhausted their significance by a long way, and we are going to look at them again. We know that one of the most, shall I say, conspicuous features of the Cherubim was their eyes, signifying their all-seeingness, their comprehensive intelligence. But let me put in here a general word about them before I go on in more particular ways. What are the Cherubim? First of all, what are they not? It ought not to be necessary to point out that they are not, as some people have foolishly asserted, angels ; nor, in fact, are they heavenly beings of any kind. Indeed, they are not actual beings at all—as actualities

they do not exist. There are no created, composite creatures which answer to this, in Heaven or earth, or in
any realm whatsoever.

The Cherubim are a symbolic representation of spiritual ideas, Divine ideas. Now of course we know that
symbols obtain in every realm, and in all times and in
all parts of the world, more perhaps in some parts than
in others. We, in our very practical Western world, still
make much use of symbols. We should not get very far
in our mathematics without them! And in many other
departments we have symbols for things. This matter of
symbolism has been very widely developed. Especially
was this true in the ancient world, where symbolism was
the common thing—everything had a symbolic representation. And God has chosen to present His eternal
truths and spiritual principles in the form of oriental
symbols. Jesus Himself presented heavenly and spiritual
truths in spoken and acted parables. John was led to
revert to the symbolic in the book of the Revelation.
Paul and Peter give spiritual principles and truths in
metaphors. The metaphors of Paul are many and
interesting, but they are means of setting forth spiritual
truths. If the Bible had first of all been written for the
modern Western world, there would have been much
less symbolism. It would have been presented in just
plain, practical statements, with little artistry or demand
upon the imagination. But it was not first of all written
in or for this modern practical Western world, and God
has chosen to use this means and this method.

But it does require the One who gave it to interpret
it. If the Holy Spirit gave Divine truths and principles
in this way, He never meant those things to be ends in
themselves. He had a meaning behind them, and only
He, the Holy Spirit, can interpret them. They cannot be
interpreted without Him. The peril is always present of
taking up these things without the Holy Spirit's interpretation, the result being mysticism. They become
fascinating as symbols and types, but they remain just
abstract ideas ; there is no practical application, there
is no spiritual result. Our business is, under the guidance
of the Holy Spirit, to extract from these symbols the
practical truth. We should see to it that we never handle
the Bible in any part without aiming at—and, by the
help of God, reaching—a practical issue. " The words
that I have spoken unto you " are—not just interesting
words, fascinating words— but " are spirit, and are life."

THE PRINCIPLES OF THE CHERUBIM
SEEN IN THE ' ACTS '

Now let us come to the Cherubim again. We have
already seen that they symbolize, amongst other things,
four main features. First, heavenly and spiritual *government* or authority in the creation, seen in the lion aspect
of the Cherubim. Secondly, heavenly and spiritual
strength, represented by the ox aspect. I know the lion
speaks of monarchy and the ox of service and sacrifice
—yes, but what is the principle in monarchy or king-

ship, and what is the principle in service and sacrifice ?
The principle of the one is government, authority ; the
principle of the other is heavenly, spiritual strength—a
kind of strength that is altogether different. In the third
place, heavenly and spiritual *intelligence*, indicated by
the man aspect of the Cherubim. And finally, the
symbol of heavenly and spiritual *sovereignty*, in the
sense of absolute liberty and freedom of movement—
the eagle. As we said earlier, an eagle on the wing is the
very embodiment of complete emancipation from earth
ties, from any kind of bondage. He just floats where he
will ; he seems to have the whole world, the whole
heaven at his command. His complete liberty of movement, absolute sovereignty in the heavens, is the symbol
of the Holy Spirit's demand for absolute sovereign
liberty, to do as He will and what He will and how He
will.

Now these are the essentials of *life*. The Cherubim
are the " living ones ", and they are the living ones
because they embody these things. If we come now to
the New Testament, and to the book of the Acts, we see
the practical expression of all this. The Man is in the
throne, and these principles are in operation in the
Church and through the Church.

Here, first of all, is the absolute authority and government of Heaven—the lion rampant. That is the book of
Acts, is it not, from one standpoint?

Again, in this book we see tremendous strength, as
of the ox, before which everything has to go down.

Whatever else may rear itself in the path or way of this, will have to yield. There is a strength here that cannot be accounted for on any earthly ground at all. The vehicles and the instruments of this strength are the ' nobodies ' of this world. They have no standing or status, no prestige, no title or reputation ; and yet through them everything is being made to yield. A hostile power does rear itself, it does assert itself, and it seems, for the moment, as though it has gained an ascendency ; but read further on—read on to the end. Here is the strength of Heaven operating in these that are nothing in this world.

As to spiritual and heavenly intelligence, it is perfectly clear in this book of the Acts. The people concerned have come into a knowledge and an understanding which is right out from Heaven. We have tried already to point out the tremendous change in their understanding. They misinterpreted, misapprehended, mistook everything up to the point of the coming of the Holy Spirit ; and then their whole outlook and mentality was revolutionized and they saw things in an entirely different way. Heavenly and spiritual intelligence has come in. And so much of the New Testament is about that, is it not? " That ye may stand . . . fully assured in all the will of God " (Col. iv. 12). " Till we all attain unto . . . the [full] knowledge of the Son of God . . . " (Eph. iv. 13).

And then, if those things are clear in the book of the Acts, the fourth thing is even more so : the absolute sovereign movement of the Holy Spirit, brooking no interference, allowing no impediment. Let there be argument, even from apostles, and the Holy Spirit will beat that down, and say: ' I demand absolute freedom from your tradition, from your interpretation, from your set ways; I demand absolute liberty to take My course. If you do not fall into line with that, then I leave you behind. I am going on.'

Now, this is all very practical. The book of the Acts is a very practical book, is it not? Here is that which is symbolized in the Cherubim actually at work and in operation. And what is the result? The inclusive result is *life*. What life! Everything is alive ; all the conditions are living. When the heavenly order and the heavenly principles are really established, then there is life. And the Cherubim represent those principles.

THE CHERUBIM IN THE GARDEN

Let us now take up the Cherubim in their various stages of presentation in the Old Testament. The first, as we know, is in the book of Genesis: "So he drove out the man ; and he placed at the east of the garden of Eden the Cherubim, and the flame of a sword which turned every way, to keep the way of the tree of life " (Gen. iii. 24). What is their place and their function here? Note three things: (a) the man is outside the garden ; (b) the tree of life is inside ; and (c) the Cherubim come between : they stand between the two

—the expelled and excluded man, and the preserved
and reserved tree of life. Now, remembering that the
Cherubim present what we may call the spiritual element in the administering of the creation—for they
always relate to the creation ; they are fourfold, and, as
we have made clear, four is the number of creation in
every respect: the four directions, the four dimensions,
the four 'elements' (earth, air, fire, water), the four
seasons, and so on—remembering this, we can see clearly that they prevent sinful and fallen man from coming
into that place of administration. He was made for that,
he was placed in the garden for that—to administer the
creation as for God, as from Heaven ; but he has sinned,
and he is expelled, and now the Cherubim, the embodiment of heavenly principles of administration, stand in
his way. They stand athwart his path ; they rule him out
of his place as God's agent in administering His creation.

For these things, these four things of which we have
spoken, are the rights and characteristics of the Spirit of
God. The rights of the Spirit of God are: heavenly
authority, government ; heavenly and spiritual strength,
a peculiar kind of strength ; heavenly and spiritual
knowledge, intelligence, understanding ; and heavenly
and spiritual liberty, freedom of movement. Now the
man has violated those very principles, those rights of
the Holy Spirit. He has sinned against the Holy Ghost,
in principle. Those very things stand in his way, across
his path and say, 'You have no place in this kingdom :
you have no authority here, you have no power here,

you have no knowledge here, you have no liberty of movement here ; you are outside, you are excluded. The kingdom is heavenly—essentially heavenly, essentially spiritual ; only spiritual men can come in here. The very laws of this spiritual kingdom debar unspiritual men from having any place.'

Now that is a statement of truth into which a very great deal of Scripture can be gathered. But, as responsible people in the work of God, we have to take serious note of these laws. And there are laws. If they had been observed, a very, very great difference would exist to-day in the Church, in Christianity. The violation of those laws has resulted in terrible, terrible disaster. *Only spiritual men and women have any place, or right, or authority, or knowledge, or liberty to touch the things of the Kingdom of Heaven.* You can see how the Gospel is gathered into this. ' You must be born of the Spirit '. " That which is born of the flesh is flesh "—and it is outside, it is excluded. " That which is born of the Spirit is spirit." So here the Cherubim—because of their very significance, because of the laws which they embody, the heavenly laws of the heavenly kingdom which they represent—stand to say very forcibly : ' Look ! You who violate heavenly principles are excluded : you are outside, and you cannot have life ; you are in death— life is not for you.'

But on the other hand, by their very position they also declare : If we are to come into the Kingdom which is characterized by *eternal* life, and to have our God-intended place of administering it—and that is what the Church is particularly called for in the ages to come ; that is the thing for which the Lord is trying to prepare us—if that is to be, the necessity is that we should be spiritual men and women. For only spiritual men—or shall we put it in the singular, only spiritual *man*—in virtue of spiritual and heavenly life, can come back to his intended function of governing for God. ' Thou madest him in order to have dominion ' (Psalm viii. 6). Yet " we see not yet all things subjected to him. But we behold . . . Jesus "—note the name *Jesus*—" . . . crowned with glory and honour " (Heb. ii. 8, 9). We see the representative One of this whole new race in the place where God intended the race to be—and where He still intends it to be.

This first presentation of the Cherubim has but one declaration : Man who is not a spiritual man is ruled out, and everything that is not governed by these heavenly and spiritual principles is outside of God's economy.

THE CHERUBIM IN THE TABERNACLE

The next presentation is in the book of Exodus, chapters xxv and xxvi. There is much about the Cherubim here in the Tabernacle, and we cannot attempt to deal with all the detail. Note, first of all, that there is a change—there is *the* change here. The Cherubim are not outside ; they are inside—they are within. Moreover they are abiding within, and they are at rest within. But note, further, that this is the priestly section of the Old Testament. The dominating features of this whole section of the Old Testament are the priest and the altar. And that explains the place of the Cherubim. The great word here is mediation : the blood of atonement, the water of purification, the oil of anointing ; and these are the things which go with the Cherubim within. They are wrought upon or into the very fabric of the curtain, the veil : the white linen, righteousness in humanity ; blue, heavenliness in humanity ; purple, royal dignity in man ; scarlet, suffering by the Man. These are the components of the Cherubim within. They cover the Mercy-seat—the place of the blood of atonement ; the place where God speaks ; the place of the covenant. It comprehends all that is meant by "a new creation *in Christ*".

Here, then, they proclaim the redemption of everything unto God—the redemption of the heavenly order, the spiritual order ; declaring that through the redemption of that heavenly order man and God are together again. The first picture is of man and God separated : God inside, so to speak, and man expelled, shut out, excluded ; a barrier between, no passing. But here the whole scene is changed : they are together. The Cherubim on the veil declare : God and man are together, in a spiritual relationship, in a heavenly order ; union has been restored, recovered. God's satisfaction has been restored to Him and everything is at rest. I suppose there was no more silent place on the earth than the place of the veil. The hush of Heaven and eternity could be felt; everything spoke of peace, of rest, of harmony.

And in relation to that the priestly ministry goes on. The ministry of the priesthood relates to that: it is the ministry of reconciliation. The first presentation of the Cherubim betokens rupture; the second proclaims reconciliation, recovery: what was lost in Genesis is found here in Exodus.

If God has a true heavenly and spiritual order, on the basis of what Christ has done by His Cross, what will happen? People will be saved! It is customary—I suppose it has to be done, and I would say even that with reservation—but it is customary to make 'special efforts', tremendous efforts to get people saved. This is no word of disparagement or criticism; it seems as though it has to be done because of the way the Church is. But mark you, if God had a Church with this heavenly nature, this spiritual nature and this heavenly order, it would be the normal thing that people are being saved all the time. " The Lord added to them . . . those that were being saved." But the Lord must have that to which He can safely add.

THE CHERUBIM IN THE TEMPLE

Here the Cherubim were:
1.   In the Oracle. I Kings vi. 23 ; II Chron. iii. 10.

2. On the walls of the House. I Kings vi. 29 ;
II Chron. iii. 7.
3. On the doors of the Oracle. I Kings vi. 32.
4. On the doors of the Temple. I Kings vi. 35.
5. On the Veil. II Chron. iii. 14.
6. On the Molten Sea. I Kings vii. 29, 36.

Two were of gold, two were of olive wood overlaid
with gold. They were frequently in pairs. Two is the
biblical symbol for full testimony, fulness of testimony.
"If two of you shall agree . . ." (Matt. xviii. 19). Two of
gold, signifying the great preciousness of that which is
here symbolized ; two of wood—olive wood overlaid
with gold—signifying humanity, strengthened by the
Holy Spirit. The olive oil, as we know, speaks of the
Spirit ; the olive tree, the strength of the Spirit in man
after God's order. Two of the Cherubim look on the
blood ; the other two compass the whole place of ministry, the place of service. Note the greatness of the two,
extending their wings to the whole width of the house.
It is not an unimportant feature. But, leaving the details,
let us sum up the meaning. What is it?

Firstly, spiritual and heavenly life in a full appreciation of Christ. Two look on the mercy-seat above the
ark, sprinkled with the precious Blood : that is, upon
Christ, God's Son, God's Man—the embodiment of
God's thoughts, the mind of the Lord, the embodiment
of God's Divine nature—in all the fulfilment of His
atoning work, all that the Cross signified in the precious
sprinkled Blood. These two bow toward that ; they are

there in the full appreciation of Christ and His mighty work by the Cross. Life comes that way, and no other way.

Secondly, heavenly principles in service. The second two are the very expression and embodiment of eager readiness to serve, to go, to obey, to respond to the slightest Divine behest. They stand ; they are not sitting. Their wings are outstretched ; they are not folded. Here, too, their feet are mentioned. Their feet are not mentioned in Genesis or in Exodus. They are mentioned in Chronicles, in Ezekiel and in Isaiah. Here it is all the active side of things ; it is service that is in view. They are the very picture and expression of this readiness to do for God—active, energetic, alert service. They look toward the place of service (II Chron. iii. 13). It is the expression of life—life in ministry, life in service—in relation to the sanctuary, in virtue of all that the Cross means.

The temple is the Old Testament figure of God's spiritual house. Peter says, " a spiritual house " of " living stones ", " to offer up spiritual sacrifices " (I Pet. ii. 5). We are that ; the Church is that. But here, too, there must be these heavenly principles that are embodied in the Cherubim, which cover all, spread out over all, govern all, embrace all. They are there in the service of *God*, in the appreciation of Christ and the understanding of Christ, the motives and principles of His own life—it is in appreciation of *that* that they are in service. The service of the House of God, therefore, must be preeminently spiritual, by spiritual men. It must be in the authority which Christ alone gives. It must be in the strength which comes from Him. It must be in the understanding and intelligence which the Spirit gives. And it must be under the absolute sovereignty of the Spirit, who says: 'Not your thoughts, not your ideas, not what you think; I must have my way, I must be free.'

So we see that it is service that is in view here in Kings and Chronicles, the great Cherubim of ministry in relation to the Cross and Christ crucified. Service is that; it is very searching.

THE PRINCIPLES IN EXPERIENCE

Now, if all this seems difficult to collect and to grasp, after all in experience it is very real. If you are going to be a true servant of the Lord, if you are really going to come into the privilege of your eternal calling, you will discover, under the hand of the Holy Spirit, these four things.

Firstly, that the authority must be with Him—the government must be upon His shoulders. And in so far as you or I take it upon our shoulders, we shall have to carry the weight of it—He will leave us to it—and it will break us. We shall find ourselves outside.

Secondly, we prove, do we not, that in this realm of things spiritual there is no human strength that can stand up to it. We need another kind of strength. When

Jesus said, " the flesh profiteth nothing ", He meant that
the strength of intellect will never get you through, the
strength of will will never get you through, the strength
of emotion will never get you through, and the strength
of the body, the best physical health and fitness, will
never get you through here ; only spiritual strength,
strength from Heaven. And in that lesson we have com-
prehended the whole Bible, in its principles of God's
way of work, God's way of service.

Thirdly, we learn in all our learning that we do not
know anything unless the Holy Spirit teaches us. One
of the very deep lessons that we have to learn in the
service of God is that, *naturally*, we know nothing! If
we think we know something—well, we are certainly in
limitation.

And finally, if there is anything that we learn at all,
it is this, that the Holy Spirit claims and demands to
have His own way. If we get in the way of the Holy
Spirit, so much the worse for us!

The way of life, of the " living ones ", is this heavenly
way where these heavenly things are true, and that is
spirituality. You say, ' Who is a spiritual person? Who
is a spiritual man or woman? Show me one!' And I
shall have to take you to one who is absolutely under
the government of the Lord in their life, one who just
refers and defers to the Lord about everything ; one who
is so conscious all the time of the necessity to draw every
bit of strength from the Lord and have no strength in
themselves ; one who is always ready to learn, and

knows so well that they know nothing, except the Lord makes it known ; and one who is giving the Lord an absolutely clear and free way to do as He likes. That is a spiritual person. And the more it is like that, the more life there will be, the greater the measure of spirituality.

Spirit and life—spirituality and livingness: these two things are linked from Genesis to Revelation. We have not yet considered the Cherubim in the book of the Revelation. When we do, we shall only find that it is the summing up of all that has gone before.

CHAPTER SEVEN

THE VICTORY OF LIFE

*" I am . . . the Living one ; and I was dead, and behold,
I am alive unto the ages of the ages, and I have the keys
of death and of Hades " (Revelation i. 17, 18).*

*" . . . In the midst of the throne, and round about the
throne, four living ones . . ." (Revelation iv. 6).*

IF YOU LOOK at those passages in their immediate
context, and in the whole context of the book of the
Revelation, you will see that they represent a tremendous triumph. Of course, the book of the Revelation,
which forms the climax of the Bible, is the book of the
ultimate triumph of the Lamb. Here is absolute victory
in every realm. But the particular connection of the
triumph, in the case both of the One who says, " I am . . .
the Living one ", and of the four living ones and all that
they represent, is, quite obviously, that of *life*. It is the
victory of life.

The statement of the Lord Himself is the statement
of an immense triumph. " I am . . . the Living one ; . . .
I was dead " (or : " I became dead "), " and behold, I
am alive unto the ages of the ages, and have the keys of

death and of Hades." That is a victory, and it is the victory of life by the Living One. The same is true in the case of the four living ones. At last we are in Heaven, at last we are in the throne! That is a tremendous victory: it is the issue of an immense and long-drawn-out conflict—the controversy of life, which began in the garden and is finished here in the Revelation.

THE CENTRAL ISSUE OF THE BIBLE—LIFE

The Bible can be divided into a number of sections, each one following in spiritual sequence upon the other, and they all, from beginning to end, centre upon that one thing, they all focus upon that one issue—life. All the trouble, all the challenge, all the controversy, all the difficulty, is about this. These different sections of the Bible are only different aspects of that one issue and that one controversy.

I.   IN THE OLD TESTAMENT

(A)   ASPECTS OF LIFE

There is first of all a short introductory section, comprising the first three chapters of the book of Genesis, introducing this whole matter of life and the controversy about it. That is the heart of the account in those chapters. What happens in the garden has to do with that life, that eternal life, and it is symbolically

presented in the *tree of life.* And so, this battle begins;
this contention has started; and it is a long-drawn-out
controversy right down the ages, all through the Bible,
until we get to the end. But the end is: the tree of life
triumphant! The life is there.

(1)   ATONEMENT: THE PRIEST

The first main section of the Old Testament, running
from the fourth chapter of Genesis to the end of
Deuteronomy, presents a new form of this same issue.
It is the test concerning life, not now in the case of
individuals, but in a collective form: firstly of the race,
and then the nation. The greater part of that section is
taken up with the record of a special forty years in the
life of Israel—the forty years in the wilderness. The
number forty, as we know, always indicates a period of
testing, probation, trial, and this section is the record of
a nation on trial in relation to the matter of life. But
here, life is connected with *atonement*; that is the central theme. The symbols of this period are the *priest* and
the *altar.* The great feast, the great sacrifice, the mercy-
seat, the sprinkled blood—all these are central. The
whole question of life focuses down upon atonement, it
rests upon atonement; and the people are on test as to
that. The end of that section finds the people in death:
the whole nation, save two, perish in the wilderness.
They have failed under the test; they have not inherited
the values of the great atoning work.

(2) AUTHORITY: THE KING

The second section runs from Joshua to Esther, and the test of life is now connected with something else. While it takes up the matter of the altar, the priest, the blood, the atonement, the predominant note and element now is that of *authority*. It begins right at the beginning of the book of Joshua, when Joshua sees a Man standing with a drawn sword, announcing himself to be the Captain of the host of the Lord, to whom Joshua is bidden to submit everything. In that moment the whole question of authority is brought in, the symbol of the period being the *throne* and the *king*, and life is connected with that. The issue of life is now bound up with Divine authority amongst the people of God. Heavenly government is established in their midst in a definite order.

(3) RECOVERY: THE PROPHET

Passing over, for the moment, the section from Job to the Song of Songs, we come to the last section of the Old Testament, from Isaiah to Malachi, which brings in another aspect of this same thing: the test of the appeal of the prophets. And what is that appeal? The nation has gone wrong: there has been departure from God, declension in the spiritual life. The appeal of the prophets is the appeal to *return* unto the Lord, and the people are tested under the appeal, the call of the prophets. The symbol here is the *prophet*, the man. And the test issues again in death, because the principle of life as therein embodied and represented has again been violated.

(B) THE CROSS BASIC TO LIFE

Now, putting all these elements together, we see that what the Old Testament teaches about the matter of life is this: that life in its fulness, as God would have it in the experience of man, rests basically upon the work of the Cross, the great sacrificial atoning and representative work of the One who became dead and is alive again. It cannot be too strongly emphasized that there is only one thing in all history that matters with God and with man, and that is the matter of eternal life. Life in its fulness, then, rests firstly upon the Cross and what the Cross means. You and I will only know that life, possess that life and increase in that life, as the Cross is a basic and primary reality in our lives, as an *applied* thing; not merely a doctrine which we accept and assent to, but something which has an *operative power* in us.

For the Cross stands over against what happened at the beginning. In the garden man's whole nature was changed. He became a different creature from what God made him and intended him to be. Everything went wrong with the man, and the man cannot be remedied, he cannot be cured. If he is to have that life which he has forfeited and missed, and from which he is now

shut out, he must die, and the new man must come in—
another man constituted according to God's mind. That
is the message of the Cross: the sin atoned for, the
sinner put out of sight, and the new man brought in.

(1) THE ALTAR

Life rests upon that for its initial reception and
possession, but it always rests upon that progressively
for its increase. We have pointed out how, in Ezekiel's
temple, the river comes down by way of the *altar*. Life
is always closely associated with the altar, and in principle it never leaves it. Just in so far as you and I have
the law of the death of Christ wrought in us, on the one
side, in that degree, and in that degree only, will the
law of the resurrection of Christ work in us, on the
other. The two things are always kept balanced. More
death means more life—deeper death, deeper life. The
Spirit of God keeps that balance, and is very practical
about it.

(2) THE THRONE

But then this matter of life does not stay there. It
rests further upon the absolute authority of the Lord in
the life, where the *throne* comes in as well as the altar
—where there is a complete subjection to the Lordship
of Christ. During the whole period of kingship, as far
as the people were concerned everything circled round

the monarchy. When that was as God meant it to be,
what life was there! Think of the last days of David and
the forty years of Solomon's reign. What a time of life!
what a time of fulness! What an object-lesson—what a
parable! What a demonstration in history of the glory
that follows when God has His throne in its place and
rightly occupied, when things are according to His mind
as to government, when the people are delighted to have
a king, and honour him as that, and are utterly subject
to him!

But when the throne becomes corrupt, when the
kingship becomes dishonoured, everything changes.
Take one illustration, so well known—King Uzziah. At
the beginning of his reign things were good, everything
was wonderful; and it continued wonderful—until
what? Until he was prospered! Oh, the peril of prosper-
ity! And then his heart was lifted up, and he became
something: self and the 'I' asserted themselves; and
the end of Uzziah, a great king, was that he died, smitten
by God with leprosy. The throne was corrupted, dragged
down into the mire. But then—" In the year that king
Uzziah died," wrote Isaiah, " I saw the Lord sitting upon
a throne, high and lifted up ". Over against the corrupt
throne, and the state of the people following suit, there
is a heavenly throne brought in. The test of life is now
connected with the throne.

Without entering into too much detail, I think it is
clear that that has a very practical application. The
government, the authority, the throne of the Lord is no

mere abstract conception and idea. It is a very practical thing, and it is brought right down into the temple, into the House of God. Life is bound up with our complete subjection to the authority of the Lord as found in His House—an exceedingly real principle. Oh, the benefits that are attached to our being subject to the Lord, in a practical way, in His House, which is His Church ; in His Temple, which is now a spiritual Body. There are tremendous blessings of life. How often does one hear people say : ' I cannot thank the Lord enough for the blessing that has come to me amongst His people '— where He is Lord. On the other hand, look at Christendom, where there is no real king and every man is doing that which is right in his own eyes. There is no authority, and no one knows what they ought to do ; it is a terrible and deplorable state. That is not life. Life is bound up with this matter of Divine authority, which is established by the Lord Himself.

And so with Israel, in this section of their history, the end was death. Even Solomon went wrong. And what tragedies followed as to the throne, and the thrones of Israel and Judah ! What a dark end to the kingly period ! —all because the throne was violated, set aside ; because the principle of authority was rejected.

(3)   THE PROPHETIC MINISTRY OF RECOVERY

Then the period of the prophets : what does it say ? It says this. Here are the men who have the message of

God to recover the people of God—to instruct them, to constitute them, to build them up, to make them a people who are in the good of the knowledge of the Lord. Perhaps we shall see this best if we move over into the New Testament.

II. IN THE NEW TESTAMENT

In the New Testament, from Matthew to Jude, we have these three elements in their spiritual counterparts, and then in the book of the Revelation all is gathered up in fulness.

(A) ASPECTS OF LIFE

(1) THE CROSS: THE PRIEST

First of all the Gospels. What is the issue of the Gospels? They have their different messages and their different aspects, but they have one issue in common: that is, the atoning Lamb offered ; Christ offered to men as the Sin-bearer, as the Sacrifice for sin ; and not only as the Sacrifice, but as men's Mediator—the Priest. And they all have to do with life : life in relation to the One who offers Himself as the Sacrifice, as the Mediator, as the Redeemer. The Cross gathers up the Gospels at last.

(2) THE THRONE: THE KING

We pass into the Acts : what do we find? The throne is introduced, and the King is on the throne: He is exalted, He is set down at the right hand of the Majesty in the heavens. The King is there. And what *life* we see in the book of the Acts because Jesus is on the throne ! The battle? Yes, terrific battle, and many battles—but victory because He is on the throne!

(3) INSTRUCTION AND RECOVERY :
PROPHETIC MINISTRY

Then, from Romans to Jude, we have everything by which the Lord's people are to be built up. All the teaching, all the instruction, all the light, all the revelation, crowded into those letters, is for building up. And it all relates to life : life based upon the Cross ; life related to the absolute authority and sovereign headship of Christ; life bound up with our growth, our development, our coming to maturity by instruction, by teaching, by the full Word given. That is the issue of all these epistles. It is a matter of life or death. That is quite obvious, for instance, in Romans, is it not? And it is true of all the others.

But let us not think that we are going to have an increase of life willy-nilly—that it is just going to happen. It will only come as we become instructed in the things of the Lord, and respond to light that the Lord gives. If the Lord's Word is there and we do not conform to it, we are strangling the very life in us. And all teaching, all instruction is intended to result in our coming into more life—it is to be *living* teaching. No

amount of teaching or meetings or conferences has any
meaning or value if there is not more life resulting from
it.

This corresponds to the prophetic section of the Old
Testament: it is to recover God's former full thought
for His people, and to bring His people into that full
thought, and, by so doing, to increase His life in them.

(B)   THE THREE BASES OF LIFE

Life, then, is based upon those three factors. Let us be
very clear about that. It is a very big thing, this matter
of life—indeed, it is *the* thing.

It rests, firstly, upon the great active reality of the
Cross in our experience.

It rests, secondly, upon the absolute sovereign headship of Christ being made very practical in our lives. It
is not just a matter of calling Jesus Christ ' Lord ': He
said that some called Him ' Lord ', and did not the things
which He said (Luke vi. 46), and that was utter hypo-
crisy. No, Lordship means absolute subjection and sub-
mission to Him, and He makes that very practical, in
many quite simple ways.

Thirdly, life, this great issue, is bound up with our
knowing all that the Lord wants us to know and that He
has provided for our knowing. Can we not confirm this,
in some measure, from our own experience? Suppose
we are waiting before the Lord with His Word, perhaps
meditating in some very familiar passage—and then,

quietly or suddenly, there comes a seeing of something
that we had never seen before, and that seeing brings
life. It *does* something! I have known that to happen
again and again as I have been meditating in the Word.
Something that I had read repeatedly has suddenly come
with a fresh force, a fresh meaning that I had not seen
before, and it is tremendously helpful. It sets the river
going, for the Lord intends it to mean life to us.

Life, then, is bound up with our knowing, and so we
have all these letters to make us know. Paul tells us
quite definitely, again and again, that the Lord's purpose
is that we should come to the full knowledge of His Son.
In our versions it is not translated like that: it generally
stands simply as ' knowledge ' ; but sometimes the Greek
word is a bigger word than our word ' knowledge '—it
is ' full knowledge ', ' acknowledgement ', ' recognition '.
There is the initial knowledge which is life. " This is
life eternal, that they may know thee the only true God,
and him whom thou didst send, even Jesus Christ "
(John xvii. 3). That is the beginning, but it is only the
beginning. There is a further, fuller knowledge, which is
far greater than that initial knowledge, and which
means much more life ; and all that is centred in these
letters.

THE REVELATION : LIFE TRIUMPHANT

And when we come to the book of the Revelation, it
is *all* there. Genesis and all else is there, all gathered up.

Every test is answered. The Devil is answered and he is
put out of court. Sin is answered by ' the Lamb that was
slain' (Rev. v. 12). Anarchy and insubjection is answered
—the King is on the throne. And the full light is shining
clearly before the throne. There are seven lamps of fire
before the throne—the seven spirits of God ; and the
four living ones, full of eyes, symbolizing all-perfect
knowledge, perfect sight, perfect revelation, are triumphant here, round the throne (iv. 5, 6). There is the
victory of the Son through the Cross ; there is the lordship of the Holy Spirit, the Spirit of life. It is all here in
the Revelation ; the whole Bible is summed up. It is now
life—life in fulness, life triumphant. The last picture
is : " He showed me a river of water of life, bright as
crystal, proceeding out of the throne of God and of the
Lamb " (xxii. 1).

THE LORD'S PEOPLE MUST EMBODY RESURRECTION

Now, in conclusion, let us bring that still nearer
home. If this is true, and not all theory, not all ideas,
then it involves us in something very great. It involves
us in this tremendous controversy, over which all the
trouble rages. If he can possibly do it, the Devil is going
to prevent men from having this life, and to strangle
and quench it in those who have it. In any way conceiv-
able to him, in his vast, diabolical wisdom, he is going to
counter this life, if he can. God is going to be triumphant at the end, but this is the battle, this is the issue now.

This, then, being the issue, and this being the testimony of Jesus, it is something in which we are involved —that that very testimony of life triumphant should be embodied in us. Do you understand that? The one issue for us, for the Church, for individual Christians, is just this: that we shall become an embodiment of the absolute triumph of Christ in resurrection—that the resurrection of the Lord Jesus should not be a part of the Christian creed, but a part of the Christian's very being. That is why the Lord has never protected His people or His Church from very, very serious adversity and opposition of every kind: for the simple reason that it is the Church and the people of God who have to embody the testimony of Jesus and be the expression of the power of His resurrection. That is why, if we are spiritual people, if we are those who are really in the way of the Lord's purpose, we have repeated and many-sided experiences of what looks like death—a final end.

PAUL'S EXPERIENCES OF LIFE OUT OF DEATH

Now, if you do not understand just what I mean, do not worry—it will come soon enough! But there are many who know all about it. Something, either in ourselves or outside of ourselves, may bring us to utter despair, to an end. If any man ever had anything to do with this matter of fulness of life, it was this man Paul—a man who could talk about resurrection as no other man. If you want to sum up all that Paul had to say, first

about the resurrection of the Lord Jesus, and then about
that resurrection as a living experience of believers, here
it is: "that ye may know what is . . . the exceeding
greatness of his power to us-ward who believe, according
to that working of the strength of his might which he
wrought in Christ, when he raised him from the dead,
and made him to sit at his right hand . . ." (Eph. i. 18 –
20).

"The exceeding greatness of his power"—in resurrection, raising Christ from the dead—"to us-ward who
believe". That is tremendous, as a statement. The man
who says things like that ought never to know anything
else. And yet that man is saying: "We despaired . . . of
life . . . We . . . had the sentence of death within ourselves . . ." Ah, but he did not leave it there. The com-
pletion of his statement is: ". . . that we should not
trust in ourselves, but in God which raiseth the dead"
(II Cor. i. 8, 9). From despair into a new experience of
resurrection; from the place where everything seemed
to be at an end and he would have to give up, into
another mighty experience of resurrection. And mark
you, this man never stopped at that experience. Right at
the end of his life, with all that he had known of the
power of His resurrection, he is still saying: "that I may
know him, and the power of his resurrection" (Phil.
iii. 10). Here is this man, who all through his life has
been in deep, terrible ways—read the catalogue of his
experiences where it looked like death (II Cor. xi. 23 –
27): "in deaths oft", he says, and he tells us how—and

yet he is the very embodiment of triumph over death—of resurrection.

Now my point is this: whether we like it or not, that is the way of the testimony; and that is why the Lord allows His people to have such experiences. That is why He has at times allowed His Church to be subjected to what has looked like the overflowing, the overwhelming of death. And yet, when it looks to have disappeared, when it looks as though Satan has absolutely triumphed and the Church is drowned, up it comes again, and not only comes up, but comes up stronger than ever. It is the old testimony about Israel in Egypt: " the more they afflicted them, the more they multiplied " (Ex. i. 12). That is the principle of resurrection: not merely resuscitation, but mighty increase. It is the Lord. Everything with God is kept in the closest relationship with this primary issue, *life*, so that it shall be manifested as what it is. It is indestructible life, and it must be manifested as that; and you and I have to be the embodiment of it, and the Church has to be the embodiment of it. That is the testimony. The testimony is not a certain set of doctrines and teachings; the testimony is, ' Jesus is alive from the dead!'

That is demonstrated in the history of God's people, from beginning to end, in many, many ways. Are you the Lord's, have you received His life? You may come more than once to the place where you despair of life, where it looks as though everything has come to an end and there is no more. But—believe it—God does not mean it as an end ; God means that there shall be more life than ever. That is His way of bringing out the testimony. It is all very well to challenge the Devil, to fight the Devil ; but do not forget that the real answer to him who is the prince of death, is laying hold on life. It is not language, it is life ; it is not phraseology, it is life ; it is not the way we attack the Devil in words, it is the life that is in us that is the answer. So the book of the Revelation sees everything that has ever come out against the Lord drawn out to its last ounce of strength, and then broken and shattered, as life rises triumphant. Yes, it is serious business : it involves in many a conflict, many an hour of distress and trial and despair ; but that is the way of the testimony of life. We should not know what this life is, if it were not set over against everything that is to the contrary. That is the testimony. So John in his letter says : " The witness (the testimony) is this, that God gave unto us eternal life, and this life is in his Son " (I John v. 11). This is the testimony : God has given unto us eternal life. The testimony is the life.

HEAVENLY FORCES IN ACTION FOR RECOVERY OF LIFE

That is the essence of all that we have been seeking to say in these meditations. For, when we have said everything, the " living ones ", with all that they symbolically represent, in their different aspects, are, after all, *living* ones. Their chief characteristic is that they are alive—they live.

Moreover they live to mighty effect. I am so glad of the significance of Ezekiel's vision in this connection ; he has greatly helped me in this matter. You see, in Ezekiel's day everything had gone wrong. The people of God had gone away from Him, repudiated Him ; they had attached themselves to other gods—idolatry was rampant ; and the glory of the Lord had gone up and removed from them. It was a terrible picture. And at that point the " living ones ", the Cherubim, come right into view.

What is there about them at this point that we do not find anywhere else? In Eden, they are stationed at the door of the garden, to guard the way to the tree of life (Gen. iii. 24). In the Tabernacle and the Temple, they are quietly reposing upon the mercy-seat, upon the veil and the curtains, and elsewhere, and it is all rest (Ex. xxv. 18, xxvi. 1, 31 ; I Kings vi. 23 ; II Chron. iii. 10, 14). But when you come to Ezekiel, they are all disturbed, they are all worked up ; they are in a turmoil, a tumult. Everything here about this vision in Ezekiel speaks of something needing to be done. There is no rest here ; it is all movement—a tremendous picture of energy. There is a spirit almost of anxious concern because of the situation. This whole matter of life has been precipitated into a terrible conflict. Here is a situation that must be met. All this that now obtains amongst the people of God must in some way be overcome, because it spells death. And so the living ones come into tremendous activity—they are all action.

I am glad it is like that: that, when things go wrong,
the Lord does not, so to speak, just sit down and give up;
say, ' It is no good, we cannot do anything about it.' That
is the time when the Lord reacts. I may be wrong, but I
have the sense that that which is represented by the living ones is getting very much into action just now. There
is a new sense of God being on the move, in relation to
the existing state of things. He would say to us, that He
is not just accepting this, He is not sitting down under
this, He is not defeated by this. This is not too much for
Him. He is going to answer ; it is not the end. The end
is going to be better than this!

Do we believe that? If we do not, we may as well give
it all up. But God is a God who is on the move, and He
is on the move with this one thing in view: the full
flood of the river of life, absolutely triumphant, in you,
in me. Over against our despair of ourselves, and the
hopelessness of things as we see them—over against it
all, however dark the picture, let us believe that God is
yet going to have, in full glow, His testimony that He
raised Jesus from the dead—and that in human vessels,
and in the great corporate vessel of His elect. The Lord
help us to believe it.

*" He that believeth on me, as the scripture hath said,
out of him shall flow*
        RIVERS OF LIVING WATER ".

SeedSowers

P.O. Box 3317
Jacksonville, FL 32206
800-228-2665
904-598-3456 (fax) www.seedsowers.com

REVOLUTIONARY BOOKS ON CHURCH LIFE

The House Church Movement (*Begier,Richey,Vasiliades,Viola*) 9.95
How to Meet In Homes (*Edwards*) 10.95
An Open Letter to House Church Leaders (*Edwards*) 4.00
When the Church Was Led Only by Laymen (Edwards) 4.00
Beyond Radical (*Edwards*) 5.95
Rethinking Elders (*Edwards*) 9.95
Revolution, The Story of the Early Church (*Edwards*) 8.95
The Silas Diary (*Edwards*) 9.99
The Titas Diary (*Edwards*) 8.99
The Timothy Diary (*Edwards*) 9.99
The Priscilla Diary (*Edwards*) 9.99
Overlooked Christianity (*Edwards*) 14.95

AN INTRODUCTION TO THE DEEPER CHRISTIAN LIFE

Living by the Highest Life (*Edwards*) 8.99
The Secret to the Christian Life (*Edwards*) 8.99
The Inward Journey (*Edwards*) 8.99

CLASSICS ON THE DEEPER CHRISTIAN LIFE

Experiencing the Depths of Jesus Christ (*Guyon*) 8.95
Practicing His Presence (*Lawrence/Laubach*) 8.95
The Spiritual Guide (*Molinos*) 8.95
Song of the Bride (*Guyon*) 9.95
Union With God (*Guyon*) 8.95
The Seeking Heart (*Fenelon*) 9.95
Intimacy with Christ (*Guyon*) 14.95
Spiritual Torrents (*Guyon*) 14.95
The Ultimate Intention (*Fromke*) 11.00

IN A CLASS BY THEMSELVES

The Divine Romance (*Edwards*) 8.99
The Story of My Life as told by Jesus Christ (Four gospels blended) 14.95
Acts in First Person 9.95

THE CHRONICLES OF THE DOOR *(Edwards)*

The Beginning 8.99
The Escape 8.99
The Birth 8.99
The Triumph 8.99
The Return 8.99

THE WORKS OF T. AUSTIN-SPARKS

The Centrality of Jesus Christ 19.95
The House of God 29.95
Ministry 29.95
Service 19.95

COMFORT AND HEALING

A Tale of Three Kings *(Edwards)* 8.99
The Prisoner in the Third Cell *(Edwards)* 5.99
Letters to a Devastated Christian *(Edwards)* 5.95
Healing for those who have been Crucified by Christians *(Edwards)* 8.95
Dear Lillian *(Edwards)* 5.95

OTHER BOOKS ON CHURCH LIFE

Climb the Highest Mountain *(Edwards)* 9.95
The Torch of the Testimony *(Kennedy)* 14.95
The Passing of the Torch *(Chen)* 9.95
Going to Church in the First Century *(Banks)* 5.95
When the Church was Young *(Loosley)* 14.95
Church Unity *(Litzman, Nee, Edwards)* 14.95
Let's Return to Christian Unity *(Kurosaki)* 14.95

CHRISTIAN LIVING

Final Steps in Christian Maturity *(Guyon)* 12.95
Turkeys and Eagles *(Lord)* 8.95
Beholding and Becoming *(Coulter)* 8.95
Life's Ultimate Privilege *(Fromke)* 7.00
Unto Full Stature *(Fromke)* 7.00
All and Only *(Kilpatrick)* 7.95
Adoration *(Kilpatrick)* 8.95
Release of the Spirit *(Nee)* 5.00
Bone of His Bone *(Huegel)* 8.95
Christ as All in All *(Haller)* 9.95

* call for a free catalog 800-228-2665